THE REAL THING

BY OLIVIA CLARE

Level Two was peach, and Cora held one, undimpled, in both hands. Had held it for seven minutes, squeezing. She'd been at Level Two for three weeks. The peaches were getting softer, and she was not improving.

"You know what I'm going to say," Abbey called from the back of the room. "You're not trying. You're not trying at all."

Now Abbey walked to the front of the room and spoke to her nine other students, in rows of brightly colored chairs. "Remarks for Cora? Comments?" No one said anything; Abbey tilted her head and let the silence breathe. Then she said: "We're all agreed."

Cora had been on the class waitlist for two years. Her agent had had to ask a special favor to get her in. What would Cora owe him? "Just please book a job," her agent said.

She squeezed that smooth little peach moon, that fucking fuzzy rock, but the skin showed no wrinkle. The moon would not give way. Next week she'd be demoted to Level One with a fleshy plum, or a firmer virgin plum, depending.

"What should she do now?" Linda asked Abbey. Linda was a talented older student. She'd had a whole stage career, a Drama Desk Award nomination, a lifetime ago. She fluffed out her red hair, parted like frizzy wings on either side of her head.

"She should practice at home," said Abbey, looking at Cora. "She should be practicing for hours."

If you made any dents, you could take the fruit with you. You could eat it. Abbey took the peach from Cora's hand and squeezed until the skin slid away from the flesh like thin peels of satin curtain.

"Was anyone timing me?" Abbey asked the students.

"Seconds," someone named Mark said. He'd just booked a soap opera. Abbey was a saint to him.

"When you can afford the one-on-one work," Abbey said to Cora, "that's when we'll really get somewhere." Abbey had been teaching the class for five years, but she'd told the class it felt like so much longer. It's amazing, time racing, she said, students getting bolder and younger. She was only forty-two, she liked to remind the class, younger than some of her students. She was tall with very dyed blond hair, and her own headshot was at least eight years old. Last week, a group from a former class—a few already somewhat successful in film—had surprised everyone in the middle of scene work. Lights were turned out, and there was Noelle Fox carrying a cake with trembling candles, and Lawrence Horn shouting, "Happy fifth anniversary!"

Cora received the discounted rate per month—it was still twice as much as her rent. This was Acting Anger for the Screen, and Abbey had made herself known because of it. The Lander School had a class for each emotion: Acting Sadness for the Screen, Acting Envy for the Screen, Acting Doubt for the Screen, Acting Cheer for the Screen. They called it "cheer," not "happiness" or "satisfaction." They called it "doubt," not "uncertainty" or "insecurity" or "agnosticism" or "loneliness." Cora thought they should call things what they were. In the Anger class, Abbey famously began with fruit. Unripe apricots, soft watermelons, hard watermelons. Cantaloupes were the most advanced level. You had to squeeze one until you bruised it, using your fingertips or palms, not your nails, *not your nails!*, or better, until the whole fruit opened and collapsed heartily upon your hand, until its innards made themselves sparkling and known. This was the great revelation, the culmination of your work. You could not thrash the fruit on the furniture. You could not thrash it against a wall or an object. It must be only you. There is, after all, only that.

Cora had no anger. She'd been told this. And even though it should have been easy for her to bruise a peach with a simple squeeze, out of anger or not, the peach would remain unblemished in her hand. She could never act angry, because she had not found the experience from her life to draw from, and she believed that. You must believe it to accept it, to change it. She was twenty-seven.

Her apartment in LA was in a house that had been split into five low-ceilinged one-bedroom units. No central air conditioning, and the hot water ran out in ten minutes. Her neighbor below, an aspiring model, said cold water was better for your skin, anyway, and she liked being woken up by another neighbor's vocal warm-ups at 5 a.m., because that meant she'd get up early. That neighbor was a very positive person. And she was healthy, from California originally. She even kept up with dental checkups. In one corner of Cora's bedroom, the wallpaper was shedding in long strips. There'd been an infestation of silverfish in the closet, so she kept everything folded and wadded in stacked suitcases. And Philip would not spend the night—he didn't feel clean there, he said. He'd told her that after their third date. Tonight he was taking her out, his treat, because he'd just wrapped the second in a series of four laundry detergent commercials he'd booked, and he wanted to celebrate. Also, he had a callback for a sci-fi horror film in Toronto. Also, he'd just paid off his Visa.

In the Spotless detergent commercial, Philip had a fake family, a wife who worked a long week and a daughter who played in the marching band. He played a stay-at-home husband—he had loads of laundry to do, and after trying many other detergents, he only trusted Spotless. The next commercial in the series would feature Philip and the family's border collie, and Philip was particularly nervous about that. "Animals and children," he said at dinner. "Everyone says they're difficult."

"You've never even worked with a kid," Cora said. They'd ordered decent champagne, and she had ordered a glass of merlot on the side. This was celebration. This was cheer, wasn't it? This was how they were happy. "Isn't your 'daughter' nineteen playing twelve?"

"I did a production of *The Music Man* in Minneapolis," he said. "So many kids. That was no joke."

"I was in that when I was nine," said Cora. "Back in Texas." She'd done community theater growing up outside of Houston, left for Los Angeles when she was eighteen.

Everyone in LA wondered where her accent was, and she always said she didn't have one, which was half-true.

Philip said, "The director told me I read like a dad on camera. I think I'd be a terrible dad. The director thinks I *am* a dad, you know. I had to tell him that."

"I can't even picture it," said Cora. Would that hurt him? Please him? She'd already told him about that day's class and Abbey. About her humiliation. She had texted him from the Lander School parking lot. Now she looked at his face—she'd hurt him a little. It was, as always, hard to tell. "Sorry. I've had a rough day."

"Didn't you tell me your stepdad kind of hated you?" he said. He often said this when he was trying to help her with her anger.

"I already used that for sadness," she said. "All of it."

"Every single thing?"

"I've been through them all."

This had begun as a trend and had never gone away. Reality TV had become so popular that people didn't want actors anymore, not in the old sense. More and more, casting directors looked for the real thing. If you were going to act something, then it had to be drawn from your life. It had to come from you, be you. This was what the Lander School taught. But it was beyond Method acting. If you used a memory for one emotion, you could not use it for another. She'd sat down with a Lander coach at the very beginning, and together they'd cataloged all of her significant childhood and early-adult events. They'd used her social media posts and medical records as a guide, and her own memory provided what it could. For homework, she wrote out a seven-thousand-word personal narrative. Her stepfather, her mother, her cat Lee-Lee. Her stepfather brought flowers home after fights. Once, her cat was injured and would let only Cora touch her. These were generic things, the coach warned her. Could she get more specific? The flowers were grocery store tulips. The cat's wound was large and bloody, near the tail. Each episode went on an index card—a summary of what had happened on the front, the appropriate emotion on the back. When they were done, Cora had a tall stack of cards to bring home with her. She could find so much in her for sadness. In the end, that was most of it, sadness and only a little joy. Jealousy. Insecurity. Wanting.

Philip would tell you that the business wasn't like this even five years ago, but he understood it, he said. Of course he did. He'd had many things happen to him in his life; there was so much he had inside of him! He would tell her this often.

"You should come to the set next week," Philip said. "I'll introduce you."

"I have class," Cora said. "And work." She and Philip worked for a caterer several nights a week—this was how they'd met—but Philip had been calling in sick. He needed to get up very early, and his face puffed, he said, if he stayed up too late. He blamed nothing on cigarettes or alcohol, only late nights. She'd finished all of her champagne and all of her wine and had ordered more sushi than Philip. She told everyone that her agent had told her to gain some weight, but that wasn't true. Her face was puckered and tired—she had her mother's face but had nothing like her mother's life.

Level One was plum. She'd managed to bruise one in class in those first days, but now she'd failed Level Two and would have to prove herself again. She practiced with a very ripe plum at home and had managed a small dent, a shadow, a ripple, but that was all. She was trying, "studying." In class, Abbey began with a short craft lecture and then asked Linda to step to the front. From the folding table of assorted fruit, Abbey took up a soft miniature watermelon. Linda walked to the center of the room, took the fruit as though it were already a trophy, stood still, paused, held a breath, then stood some more, transfixed. She was drawing from her well. She had two ex-husbands and an estranged daughter, and there it all was. There the coursing heat came. After two minutes of squeezing, the rind broke, the watermelon came apart in her hands.

Abbey began the applause. Linda came out of her trance and smiled. She fluffed her wings of hair and looked to be herself again, but who could know?

"Someone will clean that up," Abbey said. That was the job of the lowest-performing student of the day, to clean up the fruit pieces on the floor, the mush.

"That was rough," said Linda, shaking her whole body, back in this world as best as she could be. "I barely remember it."

This was what Abbey said: That when you'd found the anger, when you were in it, you couldn't describe it afterward. It all existed on some other plane.

Now there would be Cora and her plum, a beautiful new one. She walked to the front and Abbey handed over the plum—the only plum; it was meant for Cora—and Cora waited. Nine students in their chairs with their notebooks stared. Cora thought of her stepfather, the stiff tulips from Kroger, but these were meant to be drawn from only for sadness; this was cheating, and she couldn't let herself. Nothing came from the well. She thought she might pull from the periphery of some memory, a moment waiting on the side.

No, nothing. Nothing came at all.

But there was her hair. She had that, something to help her generate, get her started. She knew how to do it. She took some hair from the back of her neck and twirled its ends around her finger and pulled. She let go, and with the same hand, she made small, punctuated slaps at her cheek. The plum skin rippled, wanting to give way.

"Stop! Stop it!" Abbey called. She put a hand to her forehead and rubbed dramatically. "This is not how— No, no. That's not how we do this. You don't go to a different object and transfer the energy. It comes from *you*. And, goddamn it, you know this."

It was a trick Cora had used before, and it wasn't, as Abbey said, "Lander." One of the students smirked, and Linda just nodded.

"If there's nothing there, then play the nothing." Abbey snatched the plum from Cora and threw it into the trash. "I swear to god."

"I'm sorry," said Cora.

"Don't apologize to me," said Abbey. "Don't ever."

Cora had an audition the next day. It was for one scene in a show about forensics, and she was being questioned about a murder. She was to cry, she was to show hatred and curdling anger. Her agent was nervous for her; she sensed it on the phone. This, they both knew, was a stretch. In the waiting room outside the casting office, she sat with other young women who looked like her—just-below-average height, in their twenties or thirties, dark hair—who read their sides with moving lips, checked their phones, checked their eyelashes with a compact mirror. Philip texted Cora a photo from the detergent commercial set, his makeup-ed face filling the frame.

How could she prepare for anger? She tried to remember the face of a bully from middle school who was now a successful dermatologist. Lauren. She could try to be angry with Lauren. But Lauren had been a sad child at the root of it. How was it fair to be angry at her?

In the casting room, Cora made small talk with the casting director, who, looking at Cora's headshot and résumé, asked about the Lander School, how she liked it. "It lives up to its reputation" was what Cora always said. Then it was time. She read with the assistant, who delivered her lines in a monotone and sipped coffee from a mug that said LAGUNA BEACH in large script. When it came time for tears, Cora had them at the ready. When it came time for anger, she did not pull at her hair. She sat quietly. She waited to pull from something inside her. She waited for the inevitable piling up of all things to pile upon her and spill out. She tried again with Lauren the bully's face, but she could not remember it. Cora could remember only that she'd always felt sorry for her, and she felt no anger in that sympathy.

The assistant read Cora's cue again. "Are you going to tell us what you know?"

"You fucking wish, you fucking piece of shit" was Cora's next line. It was a bad line. A cliché line.

Nothing came. There was the sadness, the glowing, round wound of it, and that was all.

She drove to class, a mercifully short trip on the 45. Her tires were low. Her windshield was cracked. She had no money for these things, and she'd never ask anyone. For her birthday her mother had given her a beaded clutch, soft and designer, but it still sat in its velvet drawstring bag in a suitcase.

Abbey had asked her to arrive early that day. She had something waiting for Cora: a peeled hardboiled egg. It was the first time they'd had an egg in the classroom, Abbey said, and she'd boiled it herself, in her own renovated kitchen, in her own pot, on her own stove! Cora held the egg and pressed, and squeezed, and broke through until the bits spilled to the floor. Abbey said, "*Well*." Abbey said, "*Thank god*," and Cora told her, smirking, then smiling fully: "But that was sadness."

She told Philip about it at dinner, that she'd finally squeezed something, but the celebration dinner was for Philip again. He'd booked a speaking role in the movie that would shoot in Toronto. He had five lines, including "What should we do with it, boss?" and "No way."

"You wouldn't believe everything going on," he said. "I have to renew my passport. Store my car somewhere. And they keep changing the script on me." He was giddy. He was undone. "I'm unspeakably busy." She'd never heard him use the word *unspeakably* before, but she'd already witnessed him pick up words and idioms from those around him who were more successful. Oh, he was on the brink of happiness.

"Store your car?" said Cora. "It's three days."

"Street cleaning. They'll tow."

They were eating sushi again, with martinis this time, because Philip had already had champagne on his own. She didn't like martinis, but she drank them, and she didn't like sucking on the olives, but she did that too.

"Could I keep it at your place?" he said. "Your parking spot?"

"What about my car?"

"Park it on the street. You can move *your* car for street cleaning. I'll be working."

She could imagine anger unfolding within her like wings—she thought of Linda's red wings of hair. They'd have to spread, feel themselves out, keep dry, but they might be there.

"Give me your keys and I'll move it for you," she said.

"On your street? No, thanks."

"Fine. Keep it on yours. I'll come over and move it for you."

"Sounds great, love."

This is what he'd been after all along, and she'd give him a ride to the airport, too, and would help him pack. He picked up a tongue-colored piece of fish and flung it into his mouth. No, she wasn't even angry. Why not? She wished she could murder that plum.

For the next day's audition, she was to wear no makeup, and she was to use no product in her hair. There was no script, and the call was all the way out in Burbank. But she *had* put on makeup, natural makeup, had gelled back her flyaways and wavy wisps. The casting office was in a house with palms in the front and a cloudy green pool in the back. She signed in on the sheet in the living room and sat with five other women.

In twenty minutes, the assistant called Cora's name and led her to a study set up as a casting office.

"You're wearing makeup," the director said. He was the only one in the room, seated behind a cheap card table. He looked Cora's age, maybe younger. A worn leather jacket and a pretentious smile. Cora wanted to know where he'd gotten the money for a film, even just one day of shooting. Incredible. She didn't ask. The assistant took her spot behind the camera. "How old is this headshot?" The director held it in his hand. Cora had brought one, but he had everything already. That's how some of them were.

"A year."

"Really."

The assistant was already filming. "Give me a slate?" she said. And the money to employ her—where had it come from?

"Cora Ann Quinn," Cora said slowly into the camera.

"Now talk to me," the director said, leaning toward her. "Just talk. What did you eat for breakfast?"

"I didn't eat breakfast," said Cora. "I usually don't."

"Diet?"

"Money. Saves me a few dollars a day. Maybe a hundred dollars a month."

"Do you like this house?" the director said. He didn't look around. He looked at her. "It isn't mine. Don't worry."

"It's supposed to be nice, but it isn't. No one's looking after it." That's all Cora wanted to say, but this was an audition, and he wanted her to keep talking. "No one's looking after it," she repeated. "Look at the corners, that's where you can tell. Everything collects there. The walls are dusty, the outdoor plants are dying, and the indoor plants are fake. I could hear the busted pool motor from the living room. Maybe no one lives here. Upkeep is expensive."

"Say that again?" The director put a fist under his chin, concentrating. "Turn to the side."

"Upkeep is expensive."

"Now your right side."

Cora turned again. "No one lives here."

"Okay." He sat back. "Thanks very much."

Her agent called that afternoon to tell her she'd booked the job, and Cora could tell from his voice that he himself couldn't quite believe it. She'd booked only one role with him before, and that scene had been edited out of the true-crime show.

"They don't want you wearing any makeup to the set," he said. "And let your hair air-dry. It's a three-day shoot. It doesn't pay much, but it's something, at least." He sighed.

She texted Philip, who congratulated her, but he was busy packing, getting his shoes shined, buying a proper suitcase. She texted her mother, who wrote back "So proud!!!!!!" and then an image of a rose from the garden. Her mother was spending the day outside in the Texan green, wearing her gardening gloves, probably sipping tea, and suddenly that life seemed much more pleasant, healthier, than all of this desiring.

Cora *was* happy, briefly, but it was a sunken happiness, fleeting and painful. She celebrated by driving to a boutique coffee shop and purchasing a large, extravagant latte. She even chatted with the barista, found herself sharing the news, and the barista took time to scrawl "Yay" in the foam.

The script, which her agent emailed to her, was skeletal. It was a quarter of the length of a proper feature, and much of the dialogue was substituted with ellipses. "Yes, this is everything," he'd written. There wasn't much to memorize. She spent part of the weekend washing her hair and arranging it in various ways before letting it air-dry. She drove Philip to the airport at 4 a.m., and he slept most of the way. She emailed Abbey, composing and re-composing the lines in her head before she sent them. She tried hard to sound casual: "Afraid I won't be in class until Friday. I've booked a film. Thanks."

Her call time on Monday was 6 a.m., and they were filming in the Burbank house from the audition. She washed her hair and combed it in a side part, she wore no makeup, she washed her face in cold water and used a moisturizer her mother had given her, one she saved for special occasions. "Thank you," she said to the air, not knowing to what exactly, as she parked on the street. She checked in with the AD, a young woman in a zippered fleece vest—there was to be no hair or makeup, no wardrobe, and minimal lighting was being set up now. The film wasn't SAG, and there was no craft services, just a bowl of fruit, a box of donuts, a thermos of coffee. Cora took a plum and devoured it.

She waited in a bedroom with a peeling vanity and a broken ceiling fan. The young director came in with the AD.

"How're you feeling?" he said.

"Nervous," said Cora.

"Good. The scene we're about to do isn't in the script."

He was wearing the same brown leather jacket, and now, looking closer, she was sure he was younger than she was. She pictured him out with his film school friends, drunkenly yelling into the night. She pictured him having sex with a stranger. She pictured him asking his father for money.

"You're going to listen to my directions through this earpiece," he said. "I want you to just walk through the house. Like a normal person. Not like an actor. Please. Please don't be an actor."

The AD approached her and hooked something into her ear.

"When I say so," said the director, this terribly young (she thought), wealthy, fearless-for-now soul, "I want you to leave the room. And then just walk. Just walk and react."

"React to what?"

"There will be surprises. When I say so, you'll come out this door. A camera will be there."

He moved her hair from one side to the other, ruffled it a bit, then left the room with the AD. Cora went to the closed door and waited. She tried to anticipate: *surprises.* Could they hurt her on camera and get away with it? But that wouldn't make sense. The script, even in its skeletal form, was a lesbian love story. She was playing the part of a younger sister, and she had one scripted scene, a funeral scene. When were they filming *that* scene? And what was this scene? After ten long minutes, she heard the director shout from a distant room: "Stand by." Then "Rolling," then "Action."

Cora stepped out into the dark. A cameraman was there with the Steadicam strapped to his chest.

"Walk to your left," the director said in her ear. The hallway felt dusky, though it was morning. The windows had been hung with blackout curtains, and there was a light that followed Cora, though she didn't know where it came from.

"You're nervous," he said. "Be nervous."

And she was. She put her hands in front of her, feeling her way.

"Good, good," the director said in her ear. "You can talk, by the way."

"Shit," she said.

In her ear: "Good."

"I can't see anything."

"Now stop," he said. "Move to your right."

She was entering the room she'd auditioned in.

A light was on. The desk wasn't there, and the room was no longer an office. Potted plastic plants hung from the ceiling, ferns and ficus covered the floor. The windows had been boarded up. A deep buzzing sound played from a speaker hidden in the room. The camera was just behind her. "Steady," the director said. "Steady."

Someone in a cartoonish bunny mask leaped out from behind a potted lemon tree.

"Fucking dammit!" Cora shouted. "What is this?"

"Good," said the director. "Very good. Now follow them."

A red light came on in the hall. Cora followed the masked person. They were much taller, with bunny ears from the mask peeking over the top of their head. The buzzing followed her through more hidden speakers.

"Now leave them," the director said in her ear. "Go into the bedroom. The one you were just in."

She went back into the room, walked to the center, and turned, scanning. She held her arms crossed over her chest, as if in protection. The closet door opened and an unmasked man appeared.

"Run."

She ran. She could hear the man running after her. She could hear the cameraman running after her.

"You're terrified."

She was. Everything in her, she was. She thought about nothing else except getting away.

She was in the dining room, which looked out onto the pool. She hid, without being told to, beneath the table, clinging to its ornate base.

"Great! That's great."

The man came into the room, burbling and tripping over the shag carpet. Maybe he was drunk. She realized she knew nothing.

"Now," said the director. "Stand up."

Cora didn't move.

"I said stand."

This time, she stood. The man watched her and stayed where he was.

"You're incensed," said the director. "This man has wronged you. You want to tell him off. Now do it! Now say something to him."

"No," said Cora.

"Say something."

She did want to say something. What? She didn't know, couldn't think of it. She brought her hands to her face, she squeezed her cheeks. She slapped them: swift, painless slaps.

"That's good! I like that too."

Cora slapped her right cheek, harder now. The man stared at her. Said nothing. His face was smooth and indifferent. She took her hair up and twisted it. She pulled and felt a clump dislodge from her scalp.

"God, that's good," the director said. "That's so damn good."

"Fuck you," said Cora. The man stood still before her, now with a sour face.

"God, it's perfect," said the director.

She pulled at herself. She let handfuls of hair fall to the floor. "Fuck you."

* * *

Her agent called that evening to say her other scenes were delayed, but that the director was pleased, and she wouldn't be working again that week. She didn't mind that; she'd planned to take herself out to dinner that night, but instead she went to bed and fell asleep early. She showered the next morning, washed her hair, and didn't eat. She was different now. She would go to class, having booked a job, having just spent time on a set. She must look slightly altered to those around her, just as other Lander students looked to her when they'd booked something. But she wondered if they, like her, didn't feel nearly as joyous as they thought they would.

She arrived early, and Abbey was there in the large main office, signing some papers.

"I thought you weren't coming in," Abbey said.

"We filmed yesterday," said Cora. "And we'll do more next week."

"Great," said Abbey. She scanned the papers in front of her. She looked put-together and unworried. Cora couldn't imagine.

"I was angry," said Cora.

"Were you?" said Abbey. "So the class has worked for you then."

"He liked it when I tore at my hair. When I hit myself. I didn't know what to say to him. He liked it."

Abbey stood now and took off her glasses and put them

on the desk. Now she gave Cora her attention, something Cora felt she had from her so rarely. "The director?"

"Yes," said Cora. "I didn't know what to say, but it was working. What if I have to do that again?"

Cora readied herself—Abbey would rail against him, she thought, say his methods were utterly wrong.

"Well. If he liked it, he liked it," said Abbey. "That's what counts. He knows best."

"Does he?"

Cora wanted to describe him to Abbey, to tell her he looked fresh out of film school, not *Lander*. This wasn't Lander.

"Do what he says," said Abbey. "In my class, you work our way. On set, do what he says. And, you know," Abbey tapped a pen to her teeth, "people who book jobs pay an increased rate for classes."

"Seriously?"

"Depending on the job, but yes," said Abbey. "It's a Lander rule. Talk to Sheila. She'll bill you."

"But it's low-budget. I hardly talk. It's tiny."

"It doesn't matter," said Abbey. "You still pay more. Think of it this way: Would you have gotten that job without me?"

Abbey went back to her papers. Cora walked to the classroom and stopped at the door. Linda was already there, warming up her voice. "Red leather, yellow leather. Silly

Sally swiftly shooed seven silly sheep." Linda recited the words quickly, a soprano practicing her scales, running up and down the octaves, as though she was excited for something that hadn't even begun yet. A new job, a bit part on a soap or crime show, her Lander Method at work, and a line on a résumé to show for it. On the table beside Linda were watermelons, peaches, and plums. A bruised cantaloupe sat next to a peeled and shining egg.

COMA

BY A. E. STOUT

She'd fallen that morning at around 6:00 a.m. He'd managed to dial 911 before her body had started to convulse, a half dozen times, with intervals of four and a half seconds between each contortion. He'd counted carefully in case the paramedics asked. When they arrived he gave them his wife's ID and insurance card. They took her away at 6:11 a.m.

"Your wife is in a coma, Mr. Bell," the doctor said later over the phone. "She may respond, however, to your voice. It would be a good idea if you could come down here and speak to her." The hospital was two miles away—a five-minute car ride or, at his age, a forty-five-minute walk. Since Max Bell hadn't had his usual nine hours of sleep (usually he awoke at 7:00 a.m., but his wife's cries from the bathroom had awoken him an hour early that morning), he decided to lie down for another hour after speaking with the doctor.

Insistent ringing ended Max's hour-long nap, which had somehow stretched into three. It was after 10:00. Max sat up sharply in bed. He had his own room in their modest two-bedroom home. He blinked one, two, three times. He listened to the phone ringing but made no attempt to answer it. After twenty rings it stopped. Max counted them—twenty rings. Who could it have been? He hadn't any friends who would call. He had no children. No parents living. No brothers. No sisters. Strange, he thought. Ah—he remembered that his wife was in the hospital. Maybe the doctor. But why would he be calling him again? He'd already spoken to him an hour ago—and now Max looked at the clock and realized the time. Had he slept that long?

Sitting on the edge of his bed, Max studied his feet. They were good feet. Not too big. Not too small. They had served him well in his life. He'd been in the Second World War with those feet. They'd carried him across enemy lines and back home again and now he stared at them, gratefully, almost humbly, with respect. He placed them in the cotton terry slippers—navy blue—that he kept tucked underneath his bed, in the exact spot on the floor where, when he swung his legs out and over the edge of his bed in the morning, his feet landed.

Max stood up. He crossed from his room into the bath-room. Like someone who had always lived alone, he didn't bother closing the door as he relieved himself of his full morning bladder. Finished, he stood at the sink. He ran the water until it was warm; then, as it became hotter, he turned the handle on the right until the temperature was perfectly balanced to his liking. He squirted a dollop of liquid soap into his hands and rubbed them vigorously. He liked this new antibacterial type of soap because of the way it dissolved so efficiently and produced such generous suds. He liked, too, that it was antibacterial; he felt safer using this soap than he did using the plain white bars of Ivory that had been a part of his life for as long as he could remember. Once his hands were frothy with soap, Max made sure to thoroughly rinse them by rubbing them palm to palm, then the tops and sides, then clasping them under the running water in a final gesture of compliance. He kept a roll of paper towels next to the bathroom sink, preferring the singular sanitari-ness of paper to the wet bacterial breeding ground of the cotton cloth variety. He had decided that using a full sheet of paper towel was unnecessary for a single hand-washing, so he carefully tore off only half a sheet of paper towel to dry his hands. He then draped the wet half over the bathroom sink to dry, so he could use it later to wipe the counter or the toilet or to pick up toenail clippings off the floor. It took him a good three minutes to properly wash his hands.

Walking back into his bedroom, Max centered himself between the window and the bed and began his morning stretches. First, he raised both arms over his head. He looked up at the ceiling and tried to reach for it with his outstretched arms. He counted to twenty-five. Then he clasped his hands together over his head and leaned, first to the left, then to the right, ten times on each side. Next he placed his hands on his hips and twisted at the waist, ten times to the left, ten times to the right. He rolled his shoulders forward ten times, then backward ten times. He did ten neck rolls, five clockwise, five counterclockwise. He lifted his knees, first the left, then the right, as high as he could. Five times each. He used to do squats, but lately his knees had become uncooperative so now he simply raised his arms straight out in front of him and bent his knees as far as they would go, which was to say he barely bent farther than if he were sitting in a chair. He did ten of these knee bends. His whole exercise routine took exactly fifteen minutes. It was 10:27.

In the kitchen Max began to prepare his breakfast. He always ate oatmeal with a banana, sliced, and drank a cup of tea, black. He preferred the old-fashioned thick-cut oatmeal. First he poured water, one and a quarter cups perfectly measured in a Pyrex measuring cup, into a pot. He turned on a high flame, and while the water heated he measured out two-thirds of a cup of oats in an old tin measuring cup that had belonged to his mother. He returned to the stove and watched the water until it boiled. He made sure it was at a rolling boil before pouring in the oats. A small circle of bubbles appeared on the outer rim of the water. He waited until this rim of bubbles grew in size and intensity, gradually turning the entire pot into a bubbling tempest, before he turned down the flame and gently poured in the dry oats. It took four minutes for the water to come again to a rolling boil on a high gas flame. He stirred the oats in with a wooden spoon, then covered the pot and set the timer to seven minutes.

While the oatmeal cooked, Max prepared his tea. He was a Lipton man, always had been. Long as he could remember he'd drunk Lipton tea. He liked it strong. He'd boil only what he needed, just one cup of water. It took one and a half minutes for eight ounces of water to boil in a stone-cold copper teakettle. By the time the teakettle whistled and he had poured the water into his teacup and steeped the bag for five and a half minutes, his oatmeal was done cooking.

The gas flame extinguished, Max let the oatmeal sit while he sliced a ripe banana. He always saved the banana peels. Later, he would carefully hang the peel on one of the fence posts in his backyard. There, a parade of peels was on display in varying stages of decay: the brand-new bright yellow peel, the half-yellow-transforming-into-brown peel, the soft black peel, and the crispy black peel. When the crispy-black-peel stage had been achieved, Max would crumble it over the mulch pile slumped in the corner of the yard next to the trash can. He would take a shovel and turn the dirt over. Max had figured out that there were over ten thousand banana peels in the mulch pile, representing the thirty years he'd resided in his house. Earth to earth, he'd think to himself, methodically twisting the shovel handle in his hands: push, twist, dump, push, twist, dump.

After carefully scraping the oatmeal out of the pot into his white ceramic bowl, Max filled the dirty pot with water and placed it in the sink to soak. He had watched the plastics revolution swoop down upon America in the '50s and '60s and yet he'd never been seduced by plastic's convenience, price, or bright colors. While plastics had prevailed over traditional materials in most American households, Max had held firm in his use of glass and ceramic. Plastic, he knew instinctively, was suspect, not only because it was a breeding ground for bacteria but also because he disliked the texture, finding it so unappealingly inorganic that, years later, when it was proposed that plastic compounds interfered with hormone functions and were suspected to be human carcinogens, Max felt vindicated.

Max carefully arranged the slices of banana on the oatmeal and added two tablespoons of blackstrap molasses. He knew that while a medium banana has approximately 422 milligrams of potassium, two tablespoons of blackstrap molasses has 615 milligrams—the two combined were a powerful potassium topping. In the summer he might add ten to fifteen blueberries to the banana. He would alternate the fruits on top of the oatmeal—white banana, blue berry, white banana, blue berry—until he'd covered the top. He'd read that blueberries were good for improving brain function as well as the health of one's veins, and that was enough to recommend them to Max, who, before it was popular, had considered himself to be extremely health conscious. Seated at the small kitchen table, a paper napkin draped across his lap, Max ate his breakfast. He always finished the entire bowl of oatmeal and drank the whole cup of tea. Every last wet lump, every last brown drop. Once, on a morning long ago when he was a boy, his mother had served him oatmeal for breakfast when he hadn't wanted oatmeal. So he hadn't eaten it. Instead, he'd run outside and played and spent the day as boys do when they're still young and carefree. That evening, when he'd sat down for supper, his mother had placed before him the same bowl of oatmeal he'd left that morning on the kitchen table. It was cold and gummy. "Here's your supper" was all she had said. It was the Depression and food was not to be wasted. Max had learned this lesson well.

When he'd finished his breakfast, Max filled his teacup and oatmeal bowl with water and placed them next to the oatmeal pot in the sink. He then filled a glass with water and began to lay out his daily dose of vitamins: in addition to his multiple vitamin he took a calcium-magnesium supplement, garlic, vitamins E and C, fish oil, plus eight raw almonds because he'd read that they prevent cancer. He attributed his longevity, in part, to his commitment to a vitamin regime he'd engaged in long before it was commonplace. In fact, much of his spare time was spent investigating reports on vitamin therapies in health magazines, or reading books on the subject, or listening to radio programs on alternative health care. Why, he knew far more than most workers in health food stores and would often find himself educating the salespeople on the best brands of supplements, theories of absorption, and the most effective combinations of vitamins and minerals.

Max liked to arrange his vitamins according to the difficulty he had swallowing them. The larger, denser pills were placed last in a row that always began with the tiny, golden vitamin E capsule. This was a supple pill, a mere single gulp of water and it slid down his throat like a drop of saliva. Next came the garlic pill, tiny granules encased in an oblong-shaped capsule that was still small enough to go down quickly. Good for the heart, he'd think, blinking, swallowing. The multiple vitamins were the worst, and he had to take the most of these, six in all, three with breakfast and three with dinner. These pills were big and hard and bitter tasting, and when they went down sideways it hurt. He would gag and cough and sputter in an effort to avoid spitting them out. Thinking about how difficult they were to swallow inevitably caused them to go down that way, painfully. Afterward he could feel the imprint of their awkward sideways slide down his throat. His breakfast and vitamin rituals accomplished, Max left the kitchen and returned to the bedroom.

Max preferred showers to baths. The idea of soaking his body in his own floating epidermal cells and soap scum was categorically unappealing. How much better, he thought, to let the shower water wash away the dead skin cells and smells that encrusted his body. In the bathroom Max repositioned the rubber mat so it aligned with the sides of the tub. He laid the bar of soap parallel to the mat on the edge of the tub. He laid out his razor. These days Max shaved only every third day. Today he would shave. This would add an extra ten minutes to his usual forty-five-minute bathing routine. Placing a clean towel on the closed toilet seat and positioning the bath rug right next to the outside of the tub, Max removed his pajamas, folded them, placed them on the sink counter, and stepped into the tub. He watched as the water circled his feet, and here Max remembered one of the few times his feet had let him down. He'd contracted a fungus on his left foot and was required, for a period of three weeks, to keep it as dry as possible, including wrapping it in a plastic bag, securing it with tape, and hanging it outside the bathtub each time he showered. It had been an awkward three weeks. How could he, Max, who was so conscientious about his hygiene, have contracted a fungus on his foot, anyway? he'd wanted to know. Max was unimpressed when the doctor told him it was precisely overcleaning that had created the problem.

Today, for some reason, while finishing his final task in the shower, rinsing the anti-dandruff shampoo from his scalp, Max thought about the only dog he'd ever had, and that had been for less than twenty-four hours. When he was seven, his neighbor Mrs. Desmond gave him a puppy from her dog Belle's litter. She'd said he looked like he could use a dog. So he'd named it Jingle and made a bed out of an empty box and a handful of old rags, then placed it in the corner of his room, secretly knowing he'd scoop that puppy up and hold it in the crook of his arm all night long. His mother made him take Jingle back. "Dogs are dirty old things," she'd said. And that was that. From then on, throughout his adult life, he would only pet a dog with his shoe-clad foot, always releasing the thought in his mind—*dirty old dog*—without hesitation, without control, as he did so.

The last thing his mother had said when she lay dying was "You know" (he didn't think she knew who he was anymore—he had become, simply, *you*), "I think the important thing in this life is to notice things." He had never forgotten this and he had never stopped being frustrated by it. What had she meant? He'd get angry, even, remembering. What exactly was he supposed to be noticing? Max's mother had wanted her only child to become a doctor or a lawyer. He had become neither. He hadn't become a teacher or an accountant or an engineer. Mostly he had moved from job to job, selling things. He had sold insurance, shoes, encyclopedias, back when people still bought those, small and large appliances, furniture. He was sure he couldn't remember all the things he had sold in his lifetime. A lifetime of selling necessary and not-so-necessary items. He had watched his dark hairs turn gray. He had watched the landscape of his skin become peppered with brown spots and moles and could describe in remarkable detail each new spot on his hands and forearms, and the changes in pigment of the moles on his torso. He had watched gravity gradually become an overbearing and constant companion within the confines of his body, folding and slackening his flesh until he could no longer remember what it felt like to move with ease and grace and strength. Had he ever moved like that? Surely he had. He wished he could feel, just one more time, what it felt like to walk in his twenty-year-old body—just one more time.

Every day after breakfast and before lunch, Max would walk the quarter mile to the post office, where he kept a post office box. He kept all his keys on hooks screwed into the wall to the right of the front door; the post office box key was positioned just above the house key. Now, freshly showered and dressed, Max stood in front of these hooks and furrowed his brow. The post office box key was not there. He retraced his steps from the day before... Hadn't he checked the box as usual? Yes. Why hadn't he returned the key to its proper hook, as was his habit? A worried moment later, Max realized the inconvenient truth—his wife had gone to the post office yesterday a second time, late in the afternoon. The key must still be in her purse.

When the phone rang in the ICU, Max asked the nurse who picked up if she could please ask his wife where she had put the post office box key—was it in her purse? The nurse put him on hold and a few minutes later the doctor picked up the line.

"Mr. Bell, perhaps you didn't understand me when we spoke this morning. Your wife is in a coma. You can't ask her anything and she can't tell anyone anything. I know these things are upsetting, but that is the difficult reality."

"Oh, well, that is worrisome," Max heard himself say before thanking the doctor and hanging up.

He remembered his mother's neighbor calling him to say that he needed to come right away, that his mother was very, very ill. His mother lived alone in the house Max had grown up in. It was in the neighboring state, an eight-hour drive away. But Max had put it off. He had some loose ends to tie up, and it was tax season, too, so there was extra paperwork to be completed, and it was three weeks before Max made the trip. By the time he arrived, his mother was a stranger, constantly delirious or sleeping under heavy sedation.

"You should have come when I called," the neighbor had said. "Three weeks ago she would have known you, at least. What took you so long?" Max had not replied. He didn't even know this woman, this neighbor—Sally or Sarah was her name, something like that.

Standing next to the phone in its cradle, Max's nose suddenly began to drip. He moved to the bathroom, pulled five squares of toilet paper from the roll, folded them neatly like an accordion, and positioned them under his dripping nose. He watched the mucus falling softly on the tissue. He counted the drips. He counted the lapse between the drips. He will not visit her in the hospital. He won't. Instead, he will think about tomorrow, when the clock will ring, and he will sit up, swing his legs out of his bed, regard his feet, go to the bathroom, do his stretches, eat his oatmeal, drink his tea, shower and shave, hang the banana peel on the fence post, walk to the post office, and do it all over again. Counting, he is counting. The drips are slowing, three one thousand, drip, one one thousand, two one thousand, three one thousand, four one thousand, drip. He is counting the drips, he knows the number of drips, sixteen, he is counting the seconds between the drips, now four, now five, now six, he is counting the minutes until he will stop counting. He is counting and counting and counting. He is. He will sit and count and he will try to notice things. He will. Wasn't he noticing things? He was. Hadn't he been noticing things his entire life? Hadn't he been? He had.

THE END OF
THE PARTY

BY KRISTEN GLEASON

As usual, I was unimpressed with Don Meeko's wife. She was livid, pinched, and silent, and despite having nothing interesting to say about the documentary film we had just watched, she had chosen to occupy the most central position in the drawing room.

Her hair was the centerpiece. She wore it mussed, as if from an all-day sex trial.

Tony, who had lost his money, sipped his imitation tea. He was irritable. Of the six of us, he was the only one who had expected to enjoy the film.

"I didn't think they would show the actual bodies. I don't know what I thought they *would* show. Reenactments.

Their possessions. I'm no filmmaker, but I know what a film should do."

Tony had two hands, but he only ever used one. The teacup was a bit too heavy for one hand, but he refused to correct himself. Usually I forgave him for this. I called it an aesthetic constraint. But here, on the tail end of the film I had just endured, I saw his refusal for what it was: propaganda.

"And what's that?" I asked. "What is it that a film should do?"

Tony's wife, Camille, was crowding the French doors.

"Don't answer, Antonio," she said sweetly. "He's baiting you. The truth is he's a slave to his squeamishness, just like the rest of us."

"I see that you're trying to blinker me, Camille," replied Tony. His tea sloshed ruthlessly. It escaped to darken his crotch. "A film should comfort"—and here he paused; he was criminally unsure—"a film should correct. The camera should not linger on dead bodies in the surf."

"You want the coast should be clear?" said Don Meeko, and everyone groaned.

Don Meeko's wife seeped a single word. "Stupid," she said through her nose. I waved my hand around to show how much she stank. But I knew she would not relinquish her position in the center of the room. I had been at this party before.

Tony, above the clatter of his cup, pushed ahead. "The camera should show us the beds that the bodies fled before they became bodies. The beds of war. It should show us where the bodies slept so that we realize how little home can offer when there's violence about."

My wife was somewhere, enough to later count as having been in attendance. During the opening credits of the film, she'd whispered to me: *Oh! I think I know this director... psychically.*

"Irina," I had responded, "you and I are not quarantined inside of this conversation. Are you aware of that? This theater is a home theater and it is quite small and everyone can hear you, so please shut up."

Predictably, when the film ended, she had not come into the drawing room with everyone else. Perhaps she was still in the home theater. Perhaps the pantry. But what did I care where she was so long as she was quiet?

Outside on the patio, a book lay open on a big wooden table. The wind blew through its pages, and something red—a graceful little pip of color, a piece of paper with great heart—rose out of the book's middle and briefly rode the breeze and then fell onto the flagstone, where it shivered, its sides curling up.

Don Meeko, fat, with gold buttons down his chest, moved Camille from her position in front of the French doors (she resisted, that plank). Then he went through them to the outside, closing the doors behind him—as if there could be privacy from us—and stalked across the patio.

Beyond his great shoulder was the silver river, made depthless by the sun. The gentle hump of its bank was like the fat and lustful lip of the vast green countryside. Don Meeko hung in the foreground, swaying over the little red slip of paper. Then, to prove that he was our host and could do anything, he stomped the paper beneath his boot and ground it with his heel and finally snatched it up, thrusting it deep into the pocket of his vest that usually held his cigarettes.

Tony set his shaking teacup on a waist-high table and went on talking as if the scene out on the patio had not happened. "Worst of all," Tony said, "was the close-up of the wound."

"Oh, I didn't look," said Camille. She was fingering a dried rosebud that hung from the ceiling on a length of twisted twine. "I couldn't look. I knew it would be too real."

Don Meeko's wife rolled her eyes. It seemed to me that her hair had been recently heaved. It stubbornly held its interior. I counted the number of entrances into it—there were at least seven. Naturally, and grossly, I thought of Don Meeko and his role in the shape of her hair, but when I looked for him on the patio, he was no longer there.

"It was," said Tony. "It was too real, but it also made no sense. They drowned. Why should there have been a wound in a body at all? A body drowns in order to escape violence.

Drowning is what killed them. The wound misleads. The wound is beside the point."

Don Meeko came in through the library. "Use your imagination, Tony," he bellowed. He was carrying a tray of drinks. Violet-colored. Petaled glasses.

"Lover?" He offered the tray to his wife. She closed her eyes and turned her head. Said nothing. Don Meeko moved on, smiling vaguely.

Her behavior disturbed me. Her refusal—it, too, was propaganda. How had I never noticed before? I wondered about Irina but did not think of going to find her. I had become aware of the possibility of boredom, so I committed myself more completely to the conversation.

"The wound," I said, "could have come from anything. The bodies had been in the water for a long time, so the wound could have been a nibble, some sea-thing taking a bite, or the body could have come up against a bit of ocean trash, something ragged, made of metal, sharp enough to rip the flesh, which was probably fairly soft, the flesh, from soaking in that brine, if we're being real, but anyway what does it matter what happens to a body after it's dead? You know, this is what's wrong with the film. We watched it, the whole thing, and now we're thinking about the wound instead of the war. We're concerned not with the persons left behind in the beds of war, who are sleeping *inside of war* right this second, but with the corpses that escaped. There are reasons to film the living instead of the dead. The wound is not a portal. Neither is the mouth of a corpse. They don't offer us transport. Why show them at all?"

"But is a bed?" said Camille, in a needling tone. "Is a bed a portal? Isn't it?"

I was on the verge of a rant, but I noticed that Don Meeko's wife appeared to be listening to me, and I did not want to please her by losing control. She twirled a ratty bit of hair around her finger, which was so very thin, though her knuckles were swollen and red. I stood and moved toward the center of the room. As I approached, she lifted her dress very slightly and showed her shoes. She wore a strange sort of boot whose laces began at the tip of the shoe and traveled a narrow path up to and past the ankle. Her feet were monstrously long, perhaps as long as my forearm, and I drew back at the sight of them.

"What did you think of the wound?" I asked, looking through the French doors to the beyond.

Don Meeko's wife blinked slowly. Her eyes were unfocused and dim. "What did I think of the wound?" She shrugged. "It looked like an invitation... an erotic one."

Tony bowed his head. He looked deep into his imitation tea. Camille moved stiffly across the room toward her husband. When she reached him, she did not stay but, performing a fresh interest in the hanging flower she had just left, returned to the dried bud and rolled it around between her fingers as if seeing it for the first time.

"So elegant," she said. "Even with all that dust."

Don Meeko clapped. "It's that time of the afternoon," he said, "when I must remind us of how long our nights tend to go. Let's nap."

Irina was not in our bedroom, but there were traces of her everywhere: her pink and puffy clutch sat like a pound of flesh on the nightstand, the acrid melon-sweet smell of her urine lingered in the bathroom. Carelessly, she'd left her secret reading open on the bed: *You Must Try* by Dr. H. M. Trot.

I flopped onto my back and read a few lines: "Even if a full release would seem to threaten the integrity of the entrance, it must still be attempted. A rip is preferred to a repression. Take, for example, the case of the woman who spent all her time in the stables..."

I tossed the book against the wall and rolled onto my side. I tried for sleep but was pestered by thoughts of Don Meeko's wife and her preposterous hair—a trap! a labyrinth! a deflection! Clearly, I had been wounded by it, but I was not sure why. Before closing my eyes, I resolved to wake before the appointed time so as to beat her to the center of the drawing room. I would take her seat and keep it for the rest of the night's activities so as not to be forced, by the fact of her prime placement, to consider her.

A short time later, I bolted awake. The window glowed golden and rose. It was not quite evening, which meant I still had a chance. I bounded down the stairs, feeling hopeful. But when I entered the drawing room, Don Meeko's wife was already there. Perhaps she had not moved. Her eyes were dark and sagging.

"Good evening," I said.

"I hope it will be," she said. The tips of her extra-long feet stuck out from beneath the hem of her skirt like the heads of two sinister eels.

The rest of the guests filtered into the room. Tony's face wore the crease of his pillow. Camille carried a large green ledger tucked up beneath her sticklike arm. Don Meeko entered last. He sipped from an aluminum canteen, and his lips were stained cherry red. "I don't know about you," he said, "but that nap returned me to my optimism, and I don't want to hear another word about the film."

Everyone nodded their agreement, except for Don Meeko's wife, who was engaged in the difficult activity of turning her chair around without standing up. She gripped the arms of the chair and, little by little, jumping and jerking, her hair quivering but never closing, never collapsing, she managed to turn herself toward the French doors, the patio, and the still silver river beyond.

Camille sighed. "I love this time of night," she said. She wandered through the golden glow toward the French doors. She held her hands around a tiny fluttering nothing. I could see the beating of this nothing travel up through her forearm, through the little flesh she had. "I know it's obvious of me, but I used to go outside, when I was a girl. Back then there were reasons that had nothing to do with men. Reasons to be alone and to do things…"

When Camille had almost reached the doors, Don Meeko's wife stood up and began to scream. The sound was inorganic. Industrial. I covered my ears. She pointed past Camille, past the patio, to the greater outside. "A child," she said flatly. "A child was standing on the riverbank. And now I don't see him. He's fallen in. I don't see him anywhere at all."

Don Meeko rushed to her side and tried to pin her down. "Lover," he said. "Don't get up. Why would there be a child? We don't know any children."

She shook him off, then she turned to me. Gave me a withering look. "If he can't, what about you?" she said. "Can you overcome yourself? Can you leave the party? A child is drowning."

I'd never been given such explicit permission, and now I jumped at the chance to leave, however briefly. I pushed through the French doors, took the patio in three steps, and ran through the ornamental garden, kicking pebbles here and there. I stepped off the lawn and into the high grass. I felt happy out there, without them, as I'd thought I might. My knees were warm. They were following after me, I knew they would be, but I could no longer hear them.

The riverbank was sodden. The sand was dark. The river flowed swiftly along. I accepted its disregard as a matter of course.

The others arrived. Tony was out of breath. He bent at the waist and spit. Camille held back, stayed in the field. The grass was up to her waist. Her torso floated along the horizon of grass and sky. Don Meeko's wife advanced toward the water and Don Meeko grabbed at her skirt as it dragged through the wet, dark sand.

"Here," she said. "Look."

The water had nearly erased them, but they were still undeniably there: two tiny footprints.

She turned to Don Meeko. "I'm your wife," she said. "And a child has fallen into the river."

He screwed up his face. His fingers battled his run of gold buttons. He removed his vest, went to the water's edge, and flopped stomach-first into the river. He sank beneath the silvery, impenetrable surface of the water and was nowhere to be found. For the first time in years, we were without a host.

Tony pranced around. He looked thrilled. "He can't swim," he said, and Camille, who was laughing, said, "It's true. He doesn't even know how to float!"

"Well," said Don Meeko's wife, "he must try."

I went in after him. He was there, just below the surface, lying motionless in the current, but I could not lift him. I slid my hands down the length of his arms and found his fists anchored wrist-deep in the river bottom. He was holding on. I kicked his wrists until he let go, and when I lifted his head out of the water his eyes were wistful and his teeth were bared. He would not look at his wife but took some time lying on the shore before reaching, with trembling hands, for the gold buttons, for his crumpled vest.

The mood was dark. I offered to investigate the riverbank until darkness fell.

"There's no point now," said Don Meeko's wife. Her hair, in the dusky light, seemed to consist not of strands but of one single mass onto which someone had drawn a series of experimental revolutions. She brought two fingers to her forehead and pressed. Though I had not thought her capable of it, she did, in some practiced way, seem upset. "We missed the window," she said. "And I, for one, won't cling to the idea of the child's survival."

Not wanting to go back inside, I stayed to search. I waded downriver, picked my way over many submerged roots. I passed a fenced pasture, a bathtub full of trash, and two tipping gravestones that faced the river. OTHO WOODS, read one. OTHO WOODS, read the other.

When true night hit, I quickly caught a chill. As I slopped through the grass back toward the house, I said her name as a test: "Irina. Irina. Irina."

The drawing room was lively. They were playing a game of Gesture, which Don Meeko was clearly winning. But his wife was nowhere to be found. The central chair was empty. And Irina, it was just as well, was not there either.

I stood shivering between the French doors, unsure of whether or not to remove my shoes.

Beneath the dangling rose, the little red paper sat crumpled on the floor. It had escaped the considerable depth of Don Meeko's pocket sometime prior to his plunge. I pried off my wet shoes and padded across the carpet. I crouched behind the couch and smoothed the paper out. It was a list of the names of everyone in attendance. Next to Irina's name there was a question mark. Next to Don Meeko's wife's, a star.

I stood up, shivering even more. "There's a fire in the library," said Don Meeko, still gesturing hard. "I'm burning all the aromatics in the house. We've had such a hard evening. Please, go get warm."

For a long time, I stared down the hallway, unable to

decide whether to go. The library was the place of my first meeting with Irina. We had both just arrived to a long weekend at Don Meeko's. Right away, we met his new and mysterious bride, and that night, before the empty fireplace, we guessed back and forth about her:

"I hear she is critically ill."

"I heard she was involved in the Lady's Day bombing."

"Me too. I heard that, too, but she looks too young."

"Do you think she's lively enough for him? Will she know the right games?"

"Do you think… have you noticed… that she looks a bit like me?"

But this evening the library was different. It was filled with a noxious cloud of burning aromatics. Don Meeko's wife sat by the fire, her back to me, so that she did not notice my arrival. She had removed her long and curious shoes, which were drying on the hearth. She sat in a plush but armless chair, her chin against her chest. She raised her skirt and settled it across her thighs. Then she propped her left ankle on her right knee and began to tend to her foot. Her very little foot.

It was a foot that made no sense on a woman. It was both short and squat, and it lacked adult form. The sole of it had no waist. It was a child's foot, and its bottom was dark with dirt. Don Meeko's wife dampened her skirt with her spit and began to wipe the dirt away.

I looked again at her extra-long boots. Without anything in them, they had curled into something resembling the discarded skin of a snake. Slowly, silently, I left the library. I rushed through the house, looking for Irina. She was not in the pantry or the cellar or the private museum. I remembered the basement bathrooms. They sealed totally, and she so liked to be shut up. I descended the cold cement stairs and breathed deeply. Nothing. I returned to the drawing room, which was now empty. I tried the kitchen. I'd begun to think of going outside, where she most certainly would not be, when I saw a darkness floating behind the frosted glass of the conservatory door.

"Irina," I whispered.

Yes. I'm here.

"Come out."

I can't, my love. I'm marching for a cause.

"You're alone in a room," I said. The doorknob was stuck. I thought of breaking the frosted glass.

It's so beautiful, she replied. *You can't imagine. We are one large woman who has dressed to please herself.*

"Irina, you are alone in a room at Don Meeko's."

There are no men here. There are not even children. I feel like a mountain.

"Come out," I pleaded. "Let's go home. I'm tired of being a guest. And besides, the party's over."

I won't. I'll march instead. Against tyranny in every form. Don't wait for me.

"We must go. There's a game afoot. One we have not agreed to play."

We hold hands. We link arms. We aren't at all shy about touching. It's so beautiful, you can't imagine. No art. No war. No marriage. No party.

"Irina," I said, making one last attempt. "You're alone in there, and you're lonely. Please come out."

No. It's so beautiful. You can't imagine what it is to be a mountain. But try, my love. For me. You must try.

IN SEARCH OF A
BETTER ENDING

BY ANNESHA MITHA

ATTEMPT #1

He got as far as the red door.

He got as far as the red door, but he didn't knock. Instead he retraced his steps, gingerly, as if the driveway were crisscrossed with trip wires and not the swollen refuse of trees. As if he were walking away from a holy place.

He was walking away from a holy place.

My father.

My father ducked into the white Mazda, leased, that had brought him here, and, right foot dangling between accelerator and brake, he allowed it to take him back. He hadn't paid for the car in months, despite the mass of money in his bank account, owed to everyone, owed to his wife.

His apartment in North Carolina was empty. Except: Mattress. Thin sheet (forest green, my grandmother's). Toothpaste. Toothbrush. Floss. Eggs. Trader Joe's Lamb Vindaloo. Iron. Vitamin B3. Orange extension cord (a snarl, a tangle). Everything else in the purgatory of his car's trunk.

On the kitchen counter, awash in grease from the Chinese takeout he had spilled over the faux marble, was a court summons. Fourteen days ago my father had used my mother's passwords (she had changed them, but only by adding an exclamation point) to drain the money from her accounts. He knew he shouldn't have. He knew he should actually have been paying alimony, but his hand had seized when he tried to write the checks—he just couldn't bring himself to believe he deserved this. But he didn't expect his wife to fight back, to take actions that could hurt him, even land him in jail. So Uma had teeth, sharp. So she could spit in his face, her *husband's* face, her husband. My father.

My father lived in North Carolina, though the red door was in Virginia. To the red door, then back again. He was closer to death than he realized. Winston-Salem, North Carolina. Richmond, Virginia. When he was young, he would never have expected these places to mean anything to him. Even in his English-medium school in Kolkata, when he learned about the limbs and heart of America, he hadn't paid attention to the places that stewed in its belly, names that felt strange and twangy in his mouth. Like swallowing branches, like eating trees. Virginia. North Carolina.

Yes, it is possible to lose absolutely everything.

ATTEMPT #2

He got as far as the red door, but he didn't knock. He grabbed the knob, then turned. Locked. And he had thrown his keys into a gutter many weeks ago. And he was not allowed to enter. The house bloomed around the doorknob. The shutters were the same red as the door, and the windows were covered in gauzy curtains that made the house's insides look like the textured chambers of a heart. So they weren't home, his wife, his daughter. Whenever they were home, they flung the curtains open, even at night, when the whole neighborhood was dark, and anyone, any strange person, could walk the house's perimeter and gaze inside with museum eyes.

Or was it possible they were still inside? Sealed not against the neighbors' eyes but his own? Maybe they were watching him, ghosts in the windows. Maybe they were holding their breath, their words; maybe they were waiting for him to leave.

"I don't know what you're capable of," his daughter had spit at him once, after he had called every university she was accepted to and asked if they really wanted an "ungrateful girl," a "bad daughter."

My father briefly contemplated the garage door. He remembered when, during Hurricane Isabel, the power had surged and burst, trapping the car inside. He remembered lifting the door, the snap of strength in his forearms, the cobwebs and grit that clung to his fingernails. My father cracked his knuckles, felt the worm of pain in his joints. He had never been strong.

It was cold. Almost Christmas. Every other house on the block had a wreath on its door, but not his, not his wife's house. He was surprised. He'd always thought Christmas was his daughter's favorite holiday, a low-stakes holiday, celebrated quietly among family. And it *was*, but when my father came to the red door, his wife and daughter were too busy or broken to notice the chill in the air, let alone the holiday that came with it.

Standing there, my father wondered why there was no wreath, no fairy lights, and even—he squinted through the curtains—no tree? Did they hate the holiday after all?

Last Christmas had not been his best moment, he had to admit. He'd had to work, mulling over a research paper destined for an obscure publication, which he was pushing out into the world only because it represented an enormous amount of his time. He had come home full of bitterness, and his wife hadn't made the goat curry he'd demanded, and then his daughter had called down a hello to him from her room instead of running down the stairs like she used to, like she always used to. And, yes, he'd spoken more harshly than usual; and, yes, he'd slammed the door; and, no, he hadn't hit his daughter, but he'd brushed past her with a bite to his movement, so that his shoulder had pushed into hers, so her spine had hit the wall with more force than he'd intended. He hadn't intended any of it, he never had. But did he really deserve this? Weren't there fathers who were worse? Weren't there fathers who left marks in ways that he couldn't, he wouldn't?

Behind the red door was the yellow paneling of the house. He knew that in the backyard was a treehouse the previous occupants had left behind, with a ladder and bright blue swings. He could walk there if he chose. See it. Remember. Remember his daughter playing. Remember his daughter small. He didn't.

There was a sound from inside: the dog's nose snuffling at the door crack. He hadn't seen the dog in almost a year, and though she loved him best, he fought the urge to stick his finger under the bottom of the door and feel her tongue. He was not quite so pitiful yet.

It used to be better. He remembered a time when his body was nearly volcanic with joy. It was a bitter joy, the twin of power, and, yes, he knew that it made him speak sharply sometimes. But it wasn't hate like they thought it was, his wife, his daughter. If he raised his voice it was only ever for the sake of joy. Keeping it inside his body. Making it his.

He remembered how sweetly his family had followed that suburban template. The picket fence template. The PTA president template. The hikes on Sundays template. Every Fourth of July they'd leave the dog at home to howl, pack a picnic basket full of ham sandwiches and dissolving strawberries and gas station sparklers. They'd park in the inlet by the reservoir and spread out a blanket, green plaid. They'd talk to the neighbors and let their bodies blend into the grass as the sun winked once, then disappeared. My father would help his daughter climb on top of the car—the tallest she'd ever been—and watch her scream to the sky, exploding. He'd catch her, of course, if she fell, but she never did (though my father sometimes wished that she would, so he could catch her).

And though he had never been particularly affectionate with his wife, sleeping often as he did with his face crammed into the wall, he would hold her hand then, and by the glow of the fireworks would watch the other couples hold hands too. He would put his arm around her waist, he would watch his dancing daughter, he would think, I have made it I have done it and I have done it right.

At the end of the long evening, the warm skeletons of fireworks still in the sky, he drove home, calmed the sputtering dog, shoveled his daughter's warm weight into bed, listened to his wife's gentle snores, and admired how perfect his family was. The tinge of fear in his wife's eyes when he woke her to crawl into bed, oh, that was perfect, too, wasn't it? Fear is not as bad as they say. Fear means that you cannot be left. Fear means that you are together forever.

Somewhere, sometime, something went very wrong. He knew it. My father knew that while he had started out good, a good person, he was no longer good and he no longer had good things happen to him.

Was it marriage? After getting married, mornings became difficult for him. He woke up one morning with panic—unfamiliar, familiar—cresting in his throat. It felt like a fish in his esophagus—a thrashing, a drowning, a gullet full of bones. He vomited each morning into the toilet, heaving and clenching and drooling spittle on the rim. Stress, his doctor told him, anxiety, but he became convinced that there was something *in* his body, a parasite, an infection, fiddling with the controls.

If his wife heard him heaving, she didn't say anything. Only looked at him warily when he left the bathroom, wiping the filth from his mouth.

"Well?" he sometimes asked her, and he hated how aggressive his words sounded, rough and worn from the acid in his throat.

"Nothing," she always said, afraid of his voice, its potential for rising.

Even then, he hated her. He loved her, he married her, and then he hated her. His hate was a thing that lived alongside him, separate but constant. He hated how she chewed so deliberately, mincing her food between her teeth, how she left her necklaces strewn across their shared dresser, so that they interfered with his carefully organized watches and cuff links, of which there were too many because, sometimes in the late afternoon when the sky was an ache of blue, he was met with an impish desire to buy something, to choose something, many things, and make them his.

He hated, mostly, how his wife seemed to have her own private happiness, in a language totally separate from him. How she would smile to herself at parties. He wondered why he never smiled at those parties, which were torturous to him, a clash of sound and color, a terrific screech of voices. He went only because he was a part of a family, and families spend time with other families, especially here.

No, he did not see those divorce papers coming. The packet of papers was thin, but it felt heavy in his hands. When he went to his daughter's room afterward to say, "Look what your mother did to me," his daughter wore a cold mask. He could tell from the way her face settled against her skull, all tension, no give, no forgiveness, that she was the cause of the pain inside him, the lancing in his chest. At some point, he had lost her. At some point, she had chosen her mother. He imagined her in the car with his wife—*Leave him, leave him, leave him, Mom, just do it*.

Somewhere in the world was his daughter. She had a heartbeat. Teeth. Many red and mysterious organs. And: a voice. My father could not remember my voice. Somewhere in the world was my father's daughter. Somewhere in the world, but not here, not with my father as he stood in front of the red door and tried to undo undoable wrongs. My father's only daughter. Me. My name is Mrithika. My mother's name is Uma. My father's name is Tapas, and he is the only one of us no longer quite alive.

My poor, poor father. He walked away from a holy place.

ATTEMPT #3

My father got as far as the red door, but he didn't knock. On his way back to North Carolina he saw three ghosts. It is the dying who most often see the dead.

On his way back to North Carolina he stopped by a Waffle House. He hated chain restaurants, though he didn't used to. He used to go with me to the dingy Waffle House next to my middle school all the time, during those awkward years when I first began to buck his authority. On days when my father was in a good mood (a rarity, even then), he would drive me there and we would have chocolate-chip waffles with sides of bacon that floundered in their own grease.

Middle school. I changed so much in those years, stretch marks blossoming across my hips, my stomach. I slathered my body in coconut oil to get rid of them. They never relented, covering my hips as if I were an egg on the verge of cracking, as if I would one day burst from my skin.

My father didn't like that I grew. He didn't like how I became not just taller but wider. When I was alone I didn't mind my new body, how soft I felt against myself. But other people made me mind. I felt it at dance practice, when I was cast as Ganesh, when I thundered around the stage while all the other girls, still slender, gracefully bent at the waist. My mother was sick one day, so my father, knowing that there was no food at home, took me to Waffle House. And he watched me eat my pancakes with such disgust on his face.

"Why do you eat so much?" he said to me, and all the line cooks turned, hearing the venom in his voice. "You're disgusting. Don't you have any sense of control?"

We didn't go out to eat again, because soon after that day, I learned to refuse him. To speak to him in silences. To seal myself up like an unaddressed envelope.

But when my father, on the road back to North Carolina that night, saw the yellow Waffle House sign in its neon halo, he pulled over—he couldn't help himself. His car sat solitary in the lot. The restaurant was like any rest stop diner—tiles separated by grit, bar stools deflated by the heat of a million patrons, the smell of bleach and butter. There was only one person inside, an elderly white man with a grim-reaper smile, who crinkled his nose as my father entered, then turned exhaustedly to the grease souring in the pan. Without looking at him, the cook asked: "Order?"

"Chocolate-chip waffles," my father answered without thinking. He knew he could take a seat, but he stood, stretching slightly to relieve the cramping in his legs. When his plate came, he took it with burning hands and sat next to a woman in a long white sari. He was halfway through his first waffle when he realized that the woman was his dead mother. My grandmother. He was closer to death than he realized.

"Ma?" he asked. She nodded. And when she spoke it was as if the words were glad to be out of her body. They leaped out with the force of a life lived, rushing toward my father even as her hands, her face, stayed perfectly still.

She said, "Do you remember being young and spitting seeds at me while I worked in the garden?"

She said, "Do you remember me in black and white?"

She said, "Why did you choose that picture of me to put on the mantle? The one where my face is blurry, my teeth black and bent? I was beautiful once and she never knew, she'll never know, my granddaughter."

"I *liked* that picture," my father protested quietly.

"I was dying in that picture. I was dying because you let me. My boy."

His mother lifted her sari from her stomach. Her skin was ordinary, brown and swollen, but when my father leaned closer he found that he could see straight through her belly button into the mesh jelly of her inner organs. Deep inside was her pancreas, her murderer. It was full of death, putrid— the only part of her body that had been allowed to rot.

"I didn't let you die," my father replied faintly.

"A good son," said his mother, and my father shrank under her voice, "would have felt my suffering before it was spoken aloud."

My father paid at the front.

My father stepped outside the Waffle House to find that the air had grown hard in his absence. The cold forced his fingers into his palms. He rushed to his car, pulling his coat to his ears.

My grandfather's ghost was waiting in my father's car for him. He was smoking a cigarette. His nails were longer than they had been in life, and when he made a fist they curled cruelly into his skin. My father had not seen his father for ten years prior to his death, and it had been another ten years since then.

"Oh," said my grandfather when my father looked at him with a grim smile, "I didn't think you could see me."

"I don't want to see you." My father ducked into the car and started the engine, pulling out into the empty road. He tried his best to ignore the ghost next to him.

"Ten years you didn't speak to me, and I lived. Your daughter doesn't speak to you for a couple months and you're like this? I've been watching her, your daughter. Flimsy little thing. Won't make a good wife. Won't make a good mother. Won't make a good anything, really: the girl can't even do the simplest things. Did you know that she can't whistle? I watched her try, once, for an entire afternoon. Blowing air in and out of her lungs like a fish—disgusting. She thought no one was watching. But it's more pathetic if no one is watching."

My father's knuckles whitened on the steering wheel. "Don't watch my daughter."

"Well," my grandfather answered, "you can't stop me until you join me. Pathetic. Only two months and you're like this."

My father opened his mouth as if to answer, thought better of it for a moment, but couldn't help himself. "It's different for you, you know," he said to his father. "Mrithika is my only daughter. I'm not your only child."

"Only son."

"My sister cared for you far better than I did."

My grandfather laughed, his jaw loose on its hinges. "Did she? How would you know? You weren't there."

My father looked around for an exit—he'd had enough of this—but the road was unforgiving.

"You see these nails," continued my grandfather. "She never cut them."

My father glanced over at my grandfather's yellowed talons, how they pricked his palms.

"You see these hands?" my grandfather said. "These hands are what it looks like to live without love."

They drove for a long time without speaking.

"How will it happen?" asked my father, thinking about his death.

"My son," my grandfather replied, and underneath the brass of his voice there was a reluctant swell of tenderness, "that's one thing we can't tell you."

Soon after his father's ghost disappeared, my father became aware of a tightness in his gut, a hardening knot of tissue and muscle. The Waffle House's greasy pancakes had, unsurprisingly, not agreed with him, and now the churn of his stomach demanded that he pull over. A green-and-white sign loomed from behind one of the mournful hills that bordered the interstate. LAST GAS STATION FOR FORTY MILES. He swerved off, ignoring the stuttering heartbeat of his car as it protested.

The gas station was so bleak and blue that it seemed

to exist at the end of the universe. My father ran inside, past the aisles of half-bare shelves, the bottles caked with old motor oil, the festering bags of Doritos, the buffalo chicken taquitos lying corpse-like behind a glass display. He managed to plop himself down on a toilet that was very normal—relieved, finally, to be in a room without any ghosts.

Since the divorce, his stomach had begun to pain him. It felt like the pain, the pain of *missing someone*, was playing some kind of game inside of him, a clumsy children's game, Tetris or Jenga, rearranging his organs and parts. It toyed with him. He felt that when the pain finally aligned his organs just right, he would vanish—the Jenga tower, the Tetris row. Like a child's plaything, he would shatter.

How would he die? *That's one thing we can't tell you.* Maybe his pancreas would sour overnight, like his mother's had. Maybe an infection—sepsis—would thicken his bloodstream. Maybe a vein in his brain would *pop, pop, pop* or his heart would shudder shut in its cage. Maybe it would be another car, folding his soft body into the metal arms of his Mazda. As he sat on the toilet, holding his penis up from the water, crouched over with pain, he wondered if *this* would be how he died. If he would get up from the toilet and see something important in the water—a ribbon of blood, his whole stomach. But he didn't see anything, and, having relieved himself, felt better. He washed his hands.

My father, a selectively neat man, suddenly felt repulsed by the snarl of plastic bags in the passenger seat. Bags that he had accumulated from months of eating in the car, of not wanting to walk the short distance from the McDonald's parking lot to one of its many trash cans. He gathered the plastic bags and shuffled to the dumpster behind the gas station, on the lookout for more ghosts. Perched behind the dumpster was not a ghost but a dog with matted fur, peppered with fleas. She had the soft smile of the beaten. The dog cowered, her eyes twitching, and though she was a different color, and had ears that stood straight up instead of flopping over her eyes, my father was convinced he had known this dog before.

"Badam?" he asked. And why not? The ghost of his father, the ghost of his mother, why not the ghost of a dog?

The dog didn't bark, only panted weakly, releasing a gray tongue from its skull.

"Badam?" It meant "peanut" in Bengali. His mother had adopted the dog when he first left the house to live in a bachelor flat close to town to complete his PhD. She was replacing him, he felt, but he didn't mind. He liked the thought of a furred love being close to his mother, when his own love had to be so far away. Then, when his mother died, the dog died too. He liked to say it was from sadness, but the dog was fifteen and had a slow-burn kind of cancer that predated his mother's own.

"Badam?" The dog did not respond, and the dog was probably not the dog, but my father couldn't leave her there. He scooped the dog's angular body into his arms and carried her to the car, ignoring the bumps and bruises on the bottom of her belly, ignoring the fleas that leaped from her skin to his. She slumbered in the passenger seat while he drove and drove, past a hard skyline of trees, past Winston-Salem. He looked over at the dog's sleeping form and hoped beyond hope that she could cure him.

But there was no dog. And there were no ghosts. And there was nowhere in the world left for him to go.

ATTEMPT #4

He got as far as the red door, but he didn't knock. Then he drove back to his life in North Carolina. This thing called his life. His apartment didn't have air conditioning, and the heat clung to empty corners. Dried sweat rasped his armpits, his knees, everywhere sweat had a chance to gather. This, he thought. I deserve this. This loneliness. This heat.

He was already a month behind on rent. He had come here with a job. There was a reason, yes, a reason for moving. But he had lost that job the same way he had lost so many others: a slow, dripping neglect.

He had made mistakes. Many of them. He couldn't control the beast inside him, and he told himself that it was okay as long as he didn't hit them; it was okay as long as he didn't hit them; it was okay; it was okay—but he wanted to hit them, didn't he? There were days when he felt calm and dark and he could smile with his daughter, his wife; he could smile with his whole heart. And there were days when he couldn't stand them, their faces, how they contained little pieces of him. And on those days he yelled and screamed and shouted. And on those days he broke things around them so that he would not have to break them. And eventually they made their lives small for him, he knew they did, his daughter too afraid to ask him for permission to go to prom, to be with her friends, his wife slowly severing her connections in India for fear that he would overhear her speaking on the phone or, worse, that he would check the phone bill. He became their world, and eventually their lives could fit on the head of a pin. And as long as they did everything perfectly, didn't talk back or contradict or interrupt, he could maintain that calm inside himself. He could be a good husband. He could be a good father. He could be a good man.

My father sat down in the shrapnel of all this. He sat down on the mattress with the fitted sheet that kept riding up. He took his wallet out of his pocket and a picture out of his wallet. It was of the three of them and the dog, who looked anxious in his arms—she didn't like to be picked up. He had thrown away almost every reminder after it became clear that this separation was final. After it became clear that his daughter did not want to speak to him ever again. That his wife was truly not his wife. It had taken him months to realize, but when he did he stopped eating the foods that Uma made for him, he threw his wedding band into the reservoir, he shredded papers with their names on them, even important papers they might need in court. But that picture. It glued itself to him. He couldn't throw it away.

My father was closer to death than he realized.

And he remembered.

His childhood in a city made of concrete and sound.

His mother's fingers furred so softly on the knuckles.

His father's unforgiving jaw, set against the world.

His sister, her indifference, how they didn't care enough to hate each other.

Sound, light, and his wife. How when he met her she had braids that slunk down her shoulders to the top of her shaya. The birthmark on her forehead. She was already suffocating in marriage proposals when he met her, in that force-chilled lab, but she liked him, for some reason, she liked him.

The soft touch of their elbows at the Kolkata zoo, the miserable animals that surrounded them. A polar bear with its hair falling out in tufts, a ragged parrot, an elephant with rheumy eyes. And her elbow, her living skin, her smiling at him. She knew, even then, far before he did. They were in the universe together, for better or for worse.

And then the zoo dissolved into their first kiss, the latex gloves they both wore, consumed by passion after hours in their lab, a soft, gentle knocking of lips, tasting of antiseptic. Their bodies lit up by cold lasers.

And then their wedding day, how strange and bobbleheaded she looked in a face full of makeup and her street clothes, their mild, empty wedding, her family having frozen them out because they weren't meant to be married. The wet sound of a marriage document signed.

And the death in her eyes when he yelled at her for the first time, the death, the dying, her beautiful (beautiful!) deer eyes transforming into something amphibian, coldblooded, needing nothing, or nothing that he could give her.

And their basement flat in New York, barely a home, with only a curtain separating them from the laundry machines that tenants filed down the staircase to use. How, after two weeks in the harsh city, his wife, fed up, put an OUT OF ORDER sign on the washer, and when that was taken down by the landlord, she actually cut the cord. "Must have been the rats," she said, but of course they were still evicted, and they spent three shivering weeks on his work friend's couch until they could find another basement somewhere, and later, an apartment, and later, a house.

And the sex they had in that cheap motel by the Grand Canyon, on their first *real* American vacation, and how, in the months following, his wife's stomach bubbled up with a creature who was part him, all him, everything. How he ping-ponged between joy and revulsion, because after all there was a *thing inside of his wife, a thing.*

But when his daughter was born she was all human, all flesh and blood with a head full of hair and eyes shut tight against the world. And he couldn't conceive of how she would ever grow large enough to hurt him.

In his sweat-sodden North Carolina apartment, my father was closer to death than he realized. He had left holiness in another state.

My father took out his phone. First he called his wife, but she did not answer, because she was no longer his wife.

Then he called me, but I did not answer, either, though I would never stop being his daughter.

ATTEMPT #5

My father came as far as the red door, but he didn't knock.

Three miles from the red door is a brick-and-mortar T-Mobile, nestled into a nondescript strip mall like a neon dragon's egg. There are three full-time employees. One of them, Rob, works every Friday at 4 p.m., which is when, while my father was at the red door, my mother and I came with my scuffed iPhone, asking for an international plan. I was studying abroad. My mother had paid for the plane ticket on credit, never letting me know how behind we were, and years later, when I asked her why she'd let me go, why she'd suffered for me, she said: "We could finally have good things. I wanted you to have good things." Rob looked oddly stoic in his pink-and-black uniform. He told me somberly that switching to an international data plan was impossible without the permission of the plan holder, who, at that point, was still my father. I looked at my mother, who said that it was about time we let go of him, the last financial thread holding us together, the final kindness we still took from him. I changed my number then, discarding the old one like a snakeskin.

So months later, when my father called for the last time, I did not answer. I was across the ocean *having a good thing*.

Years later, at a grief group in a bland conference center, a woman who no longer had a daughter told me: "You did everything you could."

The number you have dialed has been disconnected. The number you have dialed has been disconnected. There was a ringing in my father's ears. The sound of my voice forgotten.

THE ASYLUM

BY JULIE HECHT

I finally went to check out the asylum. I went there for an appointment with the one doctor who was known as the only benzo-taper specialist. The word is *benzodiazepine* but people don't like to say long words now and they make up shorter words to use instead. What's the rush?

A filmmaker was making a film about the doctor's program to help patients taper off these addictive drugs for anxiety—drugs that they'd been given in large doses by their doctors for years. Or even just one year. No one knows how to accomplish this. If the patient stops too quickly, the patient goes crazy, has seizures, and dies. Even if the patient stops slowly, years of horrible withdrawal symptoms take place.

Among these drugs is one that a TV comedian likes to joke about almost every night—Xanax—how he needs it because of the last election in November. It's not a joke—a drug to take once or twice for emergencies, the most physiologically addictive of all benzodiazepines.

At the time I was given a prescription for some, I didn't have a computer so I couldn't google it. Had I done so, I never would have taken any. Now I google everything before making a move.

Later on, when a doctor told me he knew the chemist who invented Xanax, I was still a novice in the pharmaceutical world and said, in a mania caused by the drug, "Compliments to the chef." That's how ignorant I was.

The filmmaker wanted to film part of her project at the asylum. The people in charge there don't know much about the subject of the benzo taper; they don't care at these kinds of places. I had worked as a psychiatric aide at this particular place during a misguided work-study program in college. Not that I was interested in the subject—I just wanted to be in Cambridge with my friends and the great things of the time. Bob Dylan had hung out and performed there. Nothing could be as much fun for college students now. But they don't know that and are having empty fun all the time.

The benzo doctor worked on this program within her real job at the asylum. Her real job was giving prescriptions to patients every fifteen minutes. Then she came to realize there was an even greater need to help people get off these drugs, not on them. The patients didn't know how and while trying they suffered all kinds of miseries and destruction to their nervous systems and their lives.

I knew a former patient turned activist who knew the filmmaker, and they arranged for me to talk to this doctor. The filmmaker told me that the doctor was really into the subject of benzo tapering. The filmmaker wanted to help people understand the seriousness of the situation because she herself had been prescribed the drug Klonopin and had been wrecked and ruined by taking it and trying to stop taking it. She had tried, as many have, to stop on her own, but that drove her insane. Then she found out that she had to taper off very slowly, and she wanted to make a film about the whole subject even though it wouldn't earn money. This was her mission.

When I talked to her on the phone, I told her that it was impossible to get in touch with the doctor and she said, "Well, *I* don't know how to get in touch with her. I only know how to talk to her about the film." Then she started to get very persnickety and began to lecture me, in a shrill pitch, too, saying that I didn't need to speak with the doctor, and why didn't I do what she did and take some things like vitamin B6 and magnesium glycinate. So, she wasn't cured after all. Extreme irritability—high on the list of benzo withdrawal symptoms.

She named all these things she had done—the usual: get on a better diet, take tinctures of wild milky oat seeds, lemon balm, black walnut fresh green hulls, passionflower, hypnosis, kava. Get acupuncture, try aromatherapy, massage therapy, reflexology, homeopathy. Do aerobics, go jogging, swimming, do Pilates, yoga, and meditation. I had been a vegan almost since childhood, and all the supplements and herbal tinctures she named were ones I had tried.

Since I had a whole bunch of what are called life crises going on at the same time, I couldn't feel as good as she did. Then she told me she hadn't always felt good, and she'd felt so bad at one point she'd had to lie in bed all day—at that time this woman was young and healthy with children whom she'd driven to music and ballet lessons. She was so wrecked she couldn't do anything. But now, a few years later, after tapering off the drug completely, she was recovered and healthy again. She didn't sound so healthy to me, though, because she would always end up shrieking, "Why don't you just…," then always, do this or that.

We'd all read the manual written by the English psychiatrist Heather Ashton: "Benzodiazepines: How They Work and How to Withdraw." The manual includes all the psychological and physical withdrawal symptoms.

The former patient turned activist told me, "Some have their lives ruined completely. Some commit suicide. Others recover."

This former patient's head was filled with horror stories about people trying to taper off various benzo drugs, and she liked to tell the stories. She told me, "Some can't ever get off the medication. This is their doctors's dream, because they can keep prescribing it and don't have to hear any complaints about the horrors of tapering off."

Among the list of complaints were "excitability, jumpiness, restlessness, insomnia, nightmares and other sleep disturbances, increased anxiety, panic attacks, agoraphobia, social phobia, perceptual distortion, depersonalization, derealization, hallucinations, misperceptions, depression, obsessions, paranoid thoughts, rage, aggression, irritability, intrusive memories." During one of our phone calls, the former patient turned activist tried to remember the difference between depersonalization and derealization.

Then the physical symptoms: "headache, pain (limbs, back, neck, teeth, jaw), tingling, numbness, altered sensation, weakness ('jelly-legs'), fatigue, muscle twitches, jerks, tics, 'electric shocks,' tremors, dizziness, light-headedness, poor balance, blurred/double vision, sore or dry eyes, tinnitus."

When I was begging a doctor, "There must be someone

who can help get people off this drug," he said, with what I detected was some anger, "Don't you think I would tell you if I could unload all my benzo patients onto someone else?"

During the winter, I tried many times to reach the special benzo-taper doctor. Once when I called, I requested that the receptionist page her. The doctor called back and made an appointment and then later postponed it for an important meeting she had to attend. Doctors are always going to meetings in this new era.

One day, an ignorant secretary called me and said, "Here's the message: Dr. --------- said you have to be an inpatient and check in here at a special wing that costs fifty thousand dollars for two weeks. Because you can get seizures trying to get off these medications. You have to be here."

I told the secretary that I had been tapering off the medication under a doctor's supervision for four years and I knew how to do it without this dangerous side effect. I saw the doctor even though he was just a general doctor in Nantucket, where I lived part of the year, and he'd said that the Republican presidential candidate, the name unmentionable, was his choice in the last election.

This doctor had told me that the Democratic candidate had a body double, but I kept seeing him anyway. At first I thought he was joking, but I met someone buying vegetables at a farm and he told me that the doctor was a member of the NRA. He was a friend of the gun-toting doctor and was able to separate politics from good feelings for him.

The doctor's secretaries pretended, or actually believed, that the doctor's political statements were just a joke. They'd say, "Oh, he likes to joke around. He likes to get people all upset."

I always asked the nurse to take my blood pressure after I talked to the doctor, and it was still low-normal. That was a surprise because I had to pass pictures of guns hanging in the hallway, right outside the blood pressure–taking room.

In any case, this doctor liked guns and he told me he liked to shoot animals, including rabbits. I'm a member of PETA and I especially love rabbits. But I had to block all this out because he was the only doctor on the island who understood how the drugs worked. He once said, "Valium is a very complicated drug, which makes it extremely difficult to withdraw from. They're using it to get people off the other ones, because of its longer half-life. They're all bad in different ways—Xanax, Klonopin, Ativan."

I can barely remember how I finally got the appointment at the asylum with the filmmaker's doctor-subject. I began making plans to travel to Boston to see her. As part of my work, I wanted to photograph the nineteenth-century grand asylum buildings while I was there. My idea was to use them in my next book. When I pictured the hotel rooms where we'd be staying in Boston, I felt panic starting, especially when I thought of all the wall-to-wall carpeting. I pictured the chocolates on the beds. If my husband saw the chocolate he would gobble it up before I took it away. I called in advance and requested no radio, those electronic radios with the big flashing red numbers. Not only are they ugly, but the electromagnetic waves near your head are bad for your brain.

I had a lot of requests, and when I thought of them all, I just couldn't stand the idea of going to the hotel. I was worn out by all these details. I imagined taking out the skin lotions and creams and dental-hygiene products and putting them on the small sink counter and I imagined having to put them back in a bag. It would cause a panic to look at them again. This is one reason why I think I might be going insane. One bottle was just Dr. Bronner's liquid lavender soap.

I had to postpone my plans several times because of windstorms and the ferry cancellations from Orient Point, near my house, to Connecticut, for the next part of the trip, the long drive to Boston. Every week in March and April there was a windstorm, and even in the beginning of May the ferries were still being canceled. That's the new weather.

One of the things my husband and I fight about is travel directions. His idea is to just go. He never looks at a map or the Google directions. He doesn't use the GPS. We're always lost; we were lost before there was Google and GPS and we're just as lost now.

It was my idea to hire an inexpensive driver I knew. He was a Muslim who prayed six times a day and I was on friendly terms with him. He liked the healthiest food, but he still ate peanut butter. He wouldn't switch to almond butter.

He had short white hair and dressed in a fresh, clean dress shirt with a suit and tie. He always looked clean and healthy and told the most tedious stories about his family vacations. How they like the Poconos, how he used to be in the bagel business. That part was a shock. I'd forgotten all about it. Every time he mentioned this it was news to me. I just couldn't imagine a Muslim who prayed six times a day as someone owning a bagel business. And he talked about it as if it were completely normal, as if it were just a business, and about how his company made the best bagels in the country and I believed him.

Sometimes he'd get on the subject of even more boring things—taxes, insurance, roads, highways, alternate routes to here and there. Then I would say, "I have some work I have to do now," and put on my headphones. They were big Bose headphones; they weren't connected to anything because I hadn't learned how to do this—there was just silence. I didn't want to hear music, not even Mozart.

Once I asked a different driver if he would please turn the radio off. He said, "Don't you like music? I can play something else."

"What about playing nothing right now?" I said.

He said, "Just silence?" as if this were an incredible, new idea.

I dared to say the following sentence to my husband: "Let the driver be a present for us, that we won't fight and argue in the car about directions and getting lost." This driver never got lost. He was always looking at Google Maps. He never got into traffic. He knew every alternate route. He knew I couldn't take certain bridges or tunnels and he knew ways to avoid them. He said he had several clients who had the same requests.

The first time I tried to get ready for the trip, I realized that I hadn't unpacked all of those travel cosmetic and hygiene items left over from the last summer and fall, in Nantucket, not even counting the remedies: sea buckthorn seed oil, shea butter, aloe vera gel, un-petroleum jelly, goldenseal powder, slippery elm powder, and stinging nettle vegan capsules.

There was no way that I could organize them by myself, separating the four-month supply bag down to a week's supply. Then I saw I'd forgotten that in the kitchen there were bottles of vitamins, supplements, and tinctures. Maybe fifty of them. Maybe more. And I realized that I was in such an extreme panic that I would have to postpone the trip in order to get reorganized. I spoke to the doctor in Boston and she told me to updose the benzo by two milligrams in addition to taking CBD hemp oil five times every day instead of three times. One rule I've read, a debatable rule, is never updose.

The day came. I had decided, in advance mental preparation, that when I got to the asylum I would close my eyes because when I'd worked there it was such a beautiful, unique place. It was the most beautiful place that I could have imagined, the kind in English movies from the 1940s—for example, the asylum in the movie *Random Harvest* from 1942. The doctors and nurses in that movie were kind, not cruel, to the patients.

When I'd worked there, the grounds of the asylum near Boston were as beautiful as Central Park. I'd heard that both places had been designed by the same landscape architect, Frederick Law Olmsted, who later became a patient and lived out his life there. Lucky him. The asylum was famous for these grand old buildings from the nineteenth century and for its roster of literary and artistic patients, including Robert Lowell, Sylvia Plath, Anne Sexton, and James Taylor.

In fact, one day, when I worked there at my student job, I was walking outside from one building to another. It was spring. A guy who looked like James Taylor was sitting on a bench under a huge old tree. Later on I found out he actually *was* James Taylor. He was with a friend or another patient. They waved and asked me to come over and sit down with them. I said, "Oh, we're not allowed to socialize with patients." The James Taylor one said to me, "We don't have to pay any attention to that." They both seemed amused that anyone so young would follow rules. Trying to be good and following rules are two big mistakes that have ruined my life.

But I remembered being told in a stern way by a head nurse that things like sitting on a bench with patients were forbidden, and I'm afraid of rules, so I went on my way. I was wearing a white uniform. I had tied up my very long blond hair so I'd look less like a student. I guess that didn't work.

*   *   *

Several years ago, I read that the grounds of the asylum had been wrecked and the whole place was now just a corporate business trying to make lots of money, like most hospitals. Even though their computer page said "Harvard Medical School" as many times as they could squeeze in on one page, I didn't take it seriously—the Harvard connection—because I'd seen photographs of the place. In one photograph I saw a trash container of the same exact design and materials as I'd seen outside a King Kullen supermarket. They were a square shape, about three-by-three or more, made of a mixture of cement and pebbles. In the middle there was a plastic circle into which the trash was thrown. I also saw planters of flowers—the worst-looking flowers, probably bought at a big supermarket.

I'd seen photographs on the asylum computer site of the most expensive rooms in a once great old house for patients who didn't need psychiatric treatment but were trying to improve their lives in some other way having to do with alcohol, Ambien—those kinds of acceptable drugs. The main room was frightening, with planters of fake ivy on each end of the mantelpiece. Couldn't they get a better designer? Maybe Martha Stewart would have done it free of charge. Didn't anyone ever try to rearrange those planters?

And then there were the patients' rooms. There were photographs of royal blue swag curtain valances, and olive green wall-to-wall carpeting, and the most depressing hotel furniture from maybe the '70s, not even Ethan Allen furniture. When I worked there, the place was filled with antique institutional furniture, the kind I'd seen in old schools and old movies. They were just there from a past era of everyday beauty.

In order to go to the asylum, we had to stay at our favorite hotel in Boston. Things had changed there too. When we arrived they had music piped outside, under the beautiful Ritz-Carlton copper canopy awning—it wasn't exactly music, it was junk-pop alternating with Indian tunes for the new Taj Hotel name. I didn't yet know that the regular staff was gone. That would have been even worse to contemplate. And much worse, I had recently found out that the second concierge had died and the first one was still very seriously ill.

I'd known the first concierge a long time. You have to picture this guy. He looked like a *New Yorker* cartoon character from the old cartoons. He had a big, sloping paunch.

He wore a black suit with tails and a vest, the way the concierge people used to dress. He wore rimless rectangular glasses. He had light blue eyes and a thin mustache and he was bald. He talked in a quiet, discreet voice so that no one would know what he was doing, all the behind-the-scenes fixing of things.

He once told me that he bought his dinner on the way home at midnight. He said he was trying to lose weight to avoid being diabetic, but that he got his dinner when he "gassed up" his car, at the gas station. I'd never heard the phrase "gassed up." I tried to understand. The concierge at the Ritz-Carlton was buying his dinner at a gas station.

I said, "You know, -----, we shouldn't get food from gas stations." He said he couldn't help himself. I was looking into those strange light-blue eyes and wondering how this person could get food from a gas station. It seemed unbelievable. It's not as if I could see the answer. It would take further investigation and lots of thinking. And I can't stand thinking about the subject.

One night he said, "I'm honored to have an artist of your stature stay at the hotel."

"But, -----, Jacqueline Kennedy stayed here," I said.

"Well, she was very nice," he said without any affect other than his voice slightly going up on the words *she* and *very nice*. "But she wasn't an artist." What did it mean?

Did he disapprove of the Kennedys? After all that had happened? Compared to her, I was no one.

This was the most unbelievable sentence I'd heard anyone say about her. Later, he bought ten of my books of photographs to give as Christmas presents, and he sent them to me—he asked if I could inscribe them. He put in little notes, with a name in each one, and sent me a thank-you card for agreeing to his request.

"And around Christmastime too!" the card read. Then he added this expression that I used to hate most, before even worse ones came along: "You're the best." Now "have a good o--" and, the most horrible, "reach o--" are in the top five.

Because of the Kennedy episode, I figured the concierge might be a Republican, even though he was from Boston. On one trip, a bellman told me that I always stayed in the same room as Jacqueline Kennedy stayed in. I pictured her there in the room. What did she think of it? What about sleeping in beds that the public had slept in? Maybe someone called ahead and requested a special new mattress. The hotel, at that time, might have offered one. What about the carpet? Maybe it had been cleaned extremely thoroughly in advance of her stay. Still, they probably had scrubbed it with some toxic chemical products. Maybe it was replaced. Maybe the entire room was done over.

Then there were the pearls. I once knew two elderly white-haired ladies who worked at the antiques shop of one of the Morgan Memorial Goodwill stores in Boston. They were the managers. One had a serious Boston accent. It was fun listening to her talk about anything, for example, the casseroles her sister prepared for their dinner. The recipe contained canned cream of mushroom soup and frozen peas.

Once, we were talking about Jacqueline Kennedy and she said, "Well, we didn't like her in the beginning, but we like her better now."

I asked her why they didn't like her.

And the tinier of these ladies, who was so old she'd lost her boyfriend in World War I, said, "The way she wore her pearls inside the neckline of her dress. Things like that."

And I said, "But why? She always looked beautiful."

"Oh, I don't know," she said. "It just wasn't right. It's not traditional."

Here's what happened to the first concierge. I asked for him when I called about a room the year before, and they said he wasn't there, he was in the hospital, he was in serious condition.

I couldn't imagine going there without his being in charge at his podium.

They said he'd gone for a minor procedure—a common story—and all his organs shut down. Because he had diabetes, something went wrong with the procedure.

A bellman had once told me, "He has diabetes. And he won't lose weight or eat better or do anything to treat it."

The next time I was there the hotel doorman told me that the concierge was in a comatose state, that he wasn't expected to survive. And there was a new concierge who was only around fifty-five. This one talked about his heart problems.

How did I get into these discussions about their medical problems? I would ask them about various places in Boston and I might ask, "Are there any vegetarian restaurants?" and instead they'd tell about all the best, unhealthful restaurants in Boston.

I'd say, "We can't go there. I'm a vegan and a member of PETA." That would lead to the health benefits too. They would say they had to be careful; they had heart problems.

Then, one time I phoned and asked for the new concierge. An even newer concierge said, "He's not here anymore." And I said, "Where is he?"

"Hold on a minute," he said. He didn't say, "May I put you on a brief hold," so I knew it was something bad—he'd been fired or had quit.

Then a woman concierge got on the phone.

"We have some very sad news," she said. "----- has died."

"How could that be?" I said. I pictured him alive, with his big blue eyes. "He was only fifty-five." I remembered how he always admired the flowers I bought at Winston's to cheer up my room. He said his partner, Bill, was a flower arranger for big events.

And the woman concierge said, "He went in to have heart bypass surgery. Something went wrong and he got pneumonia. He had organ failure. And they couldn't save him."

All of a sudden, both of the concierges were gone. And all those fun conversations. I remembered this other thing about the second one. There was a store across Newbury Street—Betty something—and I'd asked him, "What was that shoe store across the street?"

"Oh, do you like their shoes?" he said. He was really interested.

And I said, "I do, because they're like shoes Rita Hayworth wore in *Gilda* and they're made of fabric."

"Yes, I think they're great too," he said.

A friendship based on these two important subjects. Lost.

Then there was the English maître d' of the dining room there. He hated the political situation but he was not supposed to talk about it. We once secretly talked about it anyway, but it didn't make us feel any better. It was one of those "But he can't win" conversations, ending with "Let's not talk about it."

Next there was the dining room. The most interesting thing that I ever saw in the hotel dining room was this scene: I was sitting at a table looking around for the quietest table, and there in the corner I saw a very old man with a long white beard. I could tell he was an Orthodox rabbi. He was dressed in all black—he was wearing a special hat.

He was dining with a man who looked like the actor Mel Gibson. This was at the height, or depth, of his anti-Semitism scandal. I thought, This is so funny to see the Orthodox rabbi dining at the old Ritz-Carlton, now the Taj, in Boston with someone who looks like Mel Gibson. I couldn't wait to tell someone about it.

I stared at these two in the corner. They were engaged in an intense conversation. They were talking seriously, I could tell that. By the time the Italian waiter came over, I realized that the man who was talking to the rabbi didn't just look like Mel Gibson—he *was* Mel Gibson.

I said to the waiter, "What are those two doing here together?"

I figured the actor was trying to make amends by asking this holy man, probably the holiest man or most important of the Jewish faith on the East Coast, how he could make amends. But I was more interested in what the rabbi was dining on at this restaurant.

"What could the rabbi have for dinner here?" I asked the waiter.

He said, "Oh, they sent over special food for him." He seemed uninterested.

I looked again and saw that everything on the table was wrapped in a large tinfoil package. He wasn't even going to use the plates or the cutlery. He was just going to unwrap the tinfoil and eat his dinner on a plate with utensils that had been sent along with the dinner. As a vegan, I understood this.

The Italian waiter didn't want to talk about it; he seemed to want to just shrug it off. Maybe there were a lot of bodyguards around.

Before or after this I never saw anything in the hotel dining room as interesting as the rabbi with Mel Gibson.

Once an American businessman was with a group and he was shouting in all the worst four-letter words. I asked the waiter, "Is this allowed, when people get drunk and talk that way?" The waiter just shrugged.

When we arrived for the asylum visit we learned that they hadn't saved the adjoining rooms I always requested. I'd told my husband for years that he had sleep apnea, and he wouldn't believe me. At last, when he began to feel tired, he went to a specialist and got a sleep-apnea mask. It's no fun walking into the bedroom and seeing him wearing that mask. The mask has a long plastic tube that fits over his nose and connects to a machine on the floor. The user's face looks like a plastic elephant trunk in a horror movie. You can never be sure the mask will work. I'm not going to even look into it. I'm tired of looking into all these things.

At the hotel they had almost all new management. The guy in charge of room-saving was a pudgy Boston boy of twenty-five. He told his age. "I'm not as young as I look," he said. He kept apologizing over and over. He kept using that word and sentence construction: "Again, I can't say how sorry I am." "Again, I don't know how this could have happened."

I finally said, "We can't just stand here all night talking about this." My husband was sitting in a chair nearby. He was enraged again and wanted to take the rooms they had saved for us. It wasn't like the scene in *Grand Hotel* where Lionel Barrymore pleads for a larger room. That was heart-wrenching.

The rooms were fine—I remember the problem—they were small and claustrophobic. And outside, in the once beautiful Boston skyline, there was a gigantic red neon sign on one of the buildings.

One room had a tiny bathroom. I couldn't decide which would be worse to have, a tiny room or a tiny bathroom. My husband hung his shirt on the fireplace screen. The fireplace screen was an antique and he covered it up by hanging his shirts on it. Why did he have to hang them on the only beautiful thing in the room?

I know why: Because it was there. That's his philosophy of life. When I say, "Why are you wearing that shirt?"—it would be a shirt that he was wearing the day before and the day before that—he would say, "Because it was there."

This was how I came to realize why he had been voted laziest boy at private school. But he never told me about that when we first met—I had to discover it myself. When I mentioned the discovery of laziness, he volunteered the information about the vote.

We had to be driven to the asylum because we'd gotten lost driving around Boston in the past.

Since the doctor hadn't given precise instructions, or any instructions, we wandered around outside trying to figure out which building to go into, then which inside door to go through. "I'm not good with directions," the doctor said when we called her. She'd already said she "wasn't good with time."

Even though it was a two-hour appointment, there wasn't enough time to tell about my years of benzo prescriptions.

The doctor acted natural, reminding me of the scene in *Take the Money and Run*, with the illegible note to the bank teller. "Act natural," or "Abt natural."

The doctor had an unusual appearance. I was surprised and glad to see her because her hair was not in any style. I knew she was busy and tired and overworked and had no time to fiddle with her hair. But her hair was thick and sort of reddish brown and short. It looked as if she had just had it chopped off and then taken a brush and brushed it away from her face and done nothing else. It was just there.

She wasn't wearing any makeup. Maybe she had put some paste foundation on her face. Or maybe that's just what her skin looked like. She had an accent. She was from an Eastern European country. Not from France or Italy. More like Slovenia. I had learned these accents from the many Bulgarians who worked in Nantucket during the summer.

The other thing I noticed was that the doctor wasn't wearing any stockings. I had to admire her for that, because it was such a hot, humid day. She was wearing no stockings and black, medium-heeled shoes, the kind that were called pumps. Black was the wrong color for the weather and for her spring dress—some hot-looking jersey with a blue, green, and yellow print. I noticed that her legs were completely white; she didn't have any sun spots or sun damage on them, even though she was middle-aged. I guessed she had spent all her time becoming a scholar and a medical expert; she didn't lie about in the sun as a young woman.

As we were leaving the appointment, I asked her, "Should I go look at the place where I was told I would stay if I came here?"

She said, "No, you don't have to look at it." She knew it wasn't going to work out, that's for sure.

"Well, I'm just curious," I said, because I'd seen the pictures. I had considered in desperation, What if I went there?

It was a disgustingly warm, humid day. The walk wasn't a short walk. But she said, "You should just walk over. I can't get in touch with the person in charge to give you any information." No one could ever get in touch with anyone at this place.

I didn't mention that the person in charge acted like a real witch and a Stepford Wife combined. I really wanted to see the rooms to see if they were as bad as they looked on the computer.

And guess what, they were. The main, small dining room was just as bad. The fake-ivy planters were still there. The head of the place started showing us things in her corporate, trained way.

I said, "Oh, I just want to see a room." She said she had only five minutes anyway. And then she said, "We don't have any open rooms—oh, yes, we do have one," and she opened the door to the room, one of the most frightening rooms you've ever seen in your life. The last patient might have run away just a few minutes before. I could feel the vibes that remained in the room.

Outside in the hallway, there a most beautiful Persian rug. I wished I could own that rug. It was a golden wheat color, the color of tall grass in the fall in Nantucket, the color of grass when the sun is shining on it right before the sunset. It had a kind of glow, like silk, even though it was a wool rug. The other colors in it were moss green and faded rose pink. I think they were small flowers and vines. Why didn't I take a photo? Afraid that Stepford woman would forbid it.

Then I looked back at the rug in the patient room. There was a used-up sisal, torn and no longer cleanable.

I asked, "Do all the rooms have these rugs?"

"Yes, I'm afraid they do," the Stepford woman said in her one moment of truth. And I said, "They should replace them. Sisal rugs aren't that expensive. They're in the Pottery Barn catalog. You could get a discount because you need so many."

"I know, I know. I'm in agreement," she said. "We discuss this all the time." A picture of those discussions at meetings flickered through my mind. "How can we make more money by inducing people to stay here?" was the theme.

I got out as fast as I could.

I wondered how this had happened to these houses. I knew how. I'd read a really good book about it, *Gracefully Insane: Life and Death inside America's Premier Mental Hospital*.

The book documented the entire downfall of this asylum and the beautiful grounds.

At the end of our appointment, the doctor had said she would talk to me for an hour every week over the phone so I wouldn't have to go all the way up there.

"I have to look at my calendar," she said. "I have three patients outside my door waiting for appointments fifteen minutes each, and I'm late. And tomorrow is a horrible day for me, but I'll email you and we can have a block of time on Friday."

I later found out from her how horrible her days were, filled with meetings, appointments, and family problems of ill health and medical disasters. When did it become a good idea for doctors to tell patients about such matters?

I called her Thursday to be sure of her plan—and she said, "Yes, I will email you." For a few hours, I believed this.

When I got home I sent her a text—her favorite way to communicate, I had to learn it—then an email, and I hate email, I can barely type, it took half an hour, asking: "What time might you have the small block of time?" I didn't really think she'd answer. And she didn't. I didn't hear from her at all.

After a few days, I called the asylum president's office to find out how I might reach the doctor. They showed no interest.

I think I once might have hung up on someone in the administrative office. It's too easy to hang up on people when talking on the iPhone. The red button calls out to be touched. *End it*, the red circle is silently saying. *It's so easy. Do it.* The idea of hanging up was inspired by the rudeness of the person who gave her first name only and said she was secretary to the president. Could that be true? "This is Jane."

I wondered what kind of a place this was, and how I might be able to get that Persian rug. I'd had a close friend in college and years later she told me that when she was in an asylum with a fireplace in the room she chipped away at the antique tiles around the fireplace. Every day she took one and when she left she had a whole collection to put in her house around her own fireplace.

But I didn't think there would be a way to get the rug, even though it was only about five-by-seven. Maybe I could offer to buy it. It was obvious that they needed money. They love money. They're a money-hungry bunch.

*   *   *

The unusual psychiatrist was smart, she was kind, but she was overworked. When she finally called back, she said she had to go out west or up north, or both, or to Abu Dhabi, to set up clinics for middle-aged people who are stuck on those drugs that their doctors gave them when they were younger. She was always traveling the world to set up clinics, since this benzo matter is a worldwide problem. At the end of the phone appointment she gave a time when she was going to call next. I didn't expect she would call, and she didn't.

Then, out of the blue, weeks later, after several emails, texts, and phone messages, she called, and said, "It was too hard with getting back, with the time change and all, from the West Coast." She kept saying, "Nowadays it's very hard to get help with this problem." I know that's true, and she said it with a true sound in her voice. It must be like *Jane Eyre* for everyone now.

She had wanted to bring in the head of the asylum to attend the first appointment. She said that he was an expert in psychopharmacology. I told her that's how I got into this situation, and that the only person I would see would be a doctor to help people get off medications, not someone whose job it was to get people on lots of drugs. I'd looked at the computer page of his biography, he was wearing a plaid suit. Isn't that what a clown wears, a plaid suit? The overworked doctor was so overwhelmed that staff people were constantly knocking on her door to tell her that she had a meeting or an appointment.

When we spoke on the phone, she would tell me, "Just one minute, someone's at the door, I have a meeting," or "Just one minute, I have five patients waiting outside." And when she opened the door the one time we were there, five patients really were outside and some kind of bureau-crat-secretary with an expression like, *I'm here to make you come to the meeting.* The person looked resigned, as if this were her job, to make the doctor come to meetings.

When we finally got outside on that humid, hot day to walk from the doctor's office to the building with the torn rugs, my husband said, "Look at the grass. They don't even maintain the grounds." And we don't care about lawns. We like open fields. That's how bad it was.

And I thought, This is very sad. Because when I worked there as a psychiatric aide, everything was so beautiful. The patients were an interesting bunch. We talked about our Marimekko dresses and we described to each other which ones we all had. A six-foot-tall, aristocratic older patient played the cello in her room. Another patient played the violin. But mostly it was sad because the grounds were designed by Frederick Law Olmsted, the one who had been there as a patient and later spent the rest of his life at the asylum after having a mental breakdown due to the extreme difficulties of his profession. I thought I'd seen this on *Biography*. It was quite interesting, the difficulties in the life of the Olmsted family and their emotional and/or psychological problems. I think that one brother married another brother's widow.

As we walked up this shabby path through the heat, humidity, and un-mowed grass, I saw that there weren't even any wildflowers. The grass had been mowed a couple of weeks ago and then only half mowed in another section. We were lucky there were no loud blowers or power mowers going at this time. But worst of all were the gray buildings called that horrible word, *condominiums*, built after the land was sold and developed to make money. Frank Lloyd Wright wanted his houses to blend into the places where he put them. Not these guys. I was looking down at the grass and my husband had to point out these so-called buildings to me.

I said, "This used to be three hundred acres or something like that. It was like a giant Ivy League college with a gigantic park."

He said, "Is that the part they sold off?"

I said, "Where?" and he pointed up to some box-style dark gray towers.

I said, "Oh, I didn't even see that. I was still looking at the grass. This is so much worse than I thought it would be." I really did think the buildings would blend into the sky or the trees in a Frank Lloyd Wright style. The trees weren't even pruned. I must say the whole place was kind of a mess.

I forgot what we were doing there at the asylum in the first place. The doctor seemed to have forgotten too. She didn't give any instructions about the benzo taper.

The whole day must have been such a shock that I'd forgotten the goal, the way shock therapy makes people lose their memories. That friend who chipped the tiles out of the asylum fireplace had been given shock therapy, and then some years later we were talking about our wasted years in college, for example, how a student had tried to seduce her by taking his pants off. This was unlike our present times, when such incidents are reported to be everyday occurrences. She couldn't remember who he was. I had to repeat his name several times, picturing him and feeling slightly sick each time. She said it was all vaguely familiar but she didn't remember anything about it. And that was sad because it was such a funny story, especially the way she told it. She'd said that at the sight of his unfortunate situation she'd thought, You must be joking.

Maybe if we met again now we could compare asylum stories. Maybe she'd remember more and we could laugh about everything.

But still, I wouldn't know what to do after we stopped laughing.

THE FAMOUS WRITER'S ASHES

BY CARLEA HOLL-JENSEN

The famous writer's ashes sit in a filing cabinet. It is a paralegal who discovers her, the award-winning author, at rest behind the hanging files.

When the paralegal brings the ashes to her employer's attention, a streak of adrenaline goes through the lawyer's body, as if someone had confronted him with evidence linking him to a long-ago crime. He's been trying to forget the ashes from the moment he first saw them. He hadn't been with the firm long when the senior partner, half-tipsy at an office party, leaned forward and with whiskey-rich breath offered to pull the famous writer out and let him have a look. That phrase—"pull her out"—gave the lawyer a thrill, like an adolescent glimpse of a forbidden magazine.

The senior partner opened the urn with a showman's flourish and the young lawyer looked down at the fine, pale powder intermingled with porous flakes of bone. The lawyer had never seen a dead body before, and had certainly never considered what it meant to cremate someone, how a person can be reduced down and down to nothing at all. He was restless for days afterward, and whenever he's thought of the ashes in the years since, he's had to distract himself. The paralegal, on the other hand, is taking it all in stride. Her mother, after all, kept one of John Wayne's molars in her pocketbook for twenty years. If anything, she seems starstruck, as though she were meeting the famous writer in the flesh.

When the paralegal suggests they display the famous writer's ashes in the waiting room, the lawyer clears his throat several times in quick succession, like a motor trying to start. He isn't sure he can walk past that urn half a dozen times a day. But the paralegal is persistent. She has a straightforward manner the lawyer finds off-putting but highly efficient. She reminds him that he has plenty of other mementos of notable clients on display in the office. What about the jersey of the athlete whose little domestic issue the lawyer was able to smooth over, or the autographed head shot of the actor whose ex-wife got nothing in the contentious divorce, thanks to him? Doesn't he think that displaying the famous writer's ashes would be a fitting tribute to another celebrated client from the firm's past?

The lawyer says he can't picture the kind of person who would actually want to see her ashes, but the paralegal assures him that there are plenty who would be interested. It's true, she admits, that the famous writer is no longer the household name she once was, but she is still a very famous writer.

In the end, the lawyer decides there is no harm in displaying the ashes. He comes to see it almost as an act of charity to recognize the accomplishments of the nearly forgotten writer. And her presence lends an air of dignity to the office, like a framed diploma or an antique vase. The urn takes pride of place in the waiting room, between a picture of the lawyer shaking hands with the former mayor and a gold record he won in a poker game from an eccentric music producer acquitted of shooting his mistress. The lawyer congratulates himself on his good judgment. How magnanimous he is, he thinks. How wise.

The urn quickly becomes an object of curiosity. Several people mistake it for a trophy and congratulate the lawyer on his victory, while others assume it is a piece of obscure art. Whatever his clients take it to be, the urn seems to elicit a dark fascination in them, drawing their gaze to it as if it were the only thing in the room. On more than one occasion, he walks into the waiting room to find a client examining their reflection in its burnished silver finish. Many people tell him of their admiration for the famous writer, reminiscing about the impact this or that novel had on them in college, or reciting to him the plots of their favorite of her stories. The lawyer always nods sagely, praising their good taste. On the rare occasion that someone asks which is his favorite, he grins ruefully and says he couldn't possibly pick. What he doesn't tell them is that he's never actually read any of the famous writer's work. He's tried to get through her collected stories a handful of times, but on each occasion, he read a few lines and then stared absently at the page for a quarter of an hour before closing the book. He prefers a good old-fashioned potboiler, especially if it's about a maverick spy or a daring, principled young law student. Nevertheless, he purchases a handsome hardcover edition of the famous writer's best-known novel and places it on the corner of his desk, just where his clients will be sure to notice it when they sit down.

The urn has not been on display long when he gets a call from a reporter from the arts and leisure section of the city paper. She's heard about the famous writer's ashes, she says, and wants to do a feature on them. She says there is a human-interest angle, a sort of "Where are they now?" for dead writers. The lawyer hesitates. He's always expected that one day he would be profiled in the paper, but not because he is the steward of a dead woman's ashes. He worries that people will draw some unseemly conclusion about him that he does not want them to consider. But the paralegal encourages him to do the interview. The famous writer deserves a little time in the spotlight after all these years, she says. And besides, she adds, it would look good for the firm. "Let everyone see how well we look after our clients," she says, "even after they're gone." Nobody is going to speculate about him, he decides. If they say anything, it will be how diligent he is, how handsome he looks in the full-color photo on the front page of the weekend edition. In the end, the lawyer concludes that one little article can't do any harm, and calls the reporter back to say he'd be happy to speak with her.

Before long, the lawyer is holding the urn like a prize pumpkin while a photographer snaps picture after picture. He can see the surface of the urn turning greasy with his fingerprints, and the thought of the ashes so close to his own flesh makes him break out in a sweat. He smiles and turns his head just slightly toward the light and smiles again as the photographer commands, but all he's thinking of is the urn in his hands and the ashes inside, and how they used to be a woman and now are not. What would happen, he wonders, if he spilled them out onto the carpet? Once they were in the air, it would be impossible to avoid breathing a little bit of them in, tasting them on his tongue.

The reporter is a lean, stylish woman who asks her questions with an attitude of flirtatious indifference. When they're done with the interview, she agrees to stay and have a drink with him in his office, and then another, and then, after everyone else has gone for the day, she agrees to let him fuck her on her hands and knees on the waiting room floor. He imagines fucking her hard enough to tip the famous writer's urn from its shelf and spill its contents all over them. At the thought of the ashes drifting down onto their bare skin, he spends himself with a start on the inside of the reporter's thigh. Afterward, the reporter makes a vague noise of assent when he suggests they had a nice time, and agrees to give him her number, though her gaze does not lift from her phone.

The story appears a few days later, wedged between a book review and a profile of an exiled artist the lawyer has never heard of. He worries he looks stiff and charmless in the photo, but when he arrives at work the next morning, the paralegal assures him that he and the ashes have made quite the impression. She informs him that the answering machine was completely full when she got in. A few of the messages, she admits, are not complimentary, but she's already compiled a list of the interview requests he's received. The famous writer is, once again, a sensation, and now so is he.

He gives more interviews. He appears on public radio. The paralegal supplies him with briefs as if he were going to court. Though she was already familiar with the details of the famous writer's life, the paralegal takes it upon herself to read several biographies, as well as her edited diaries and her unpublished papers that the firm has retained in its capacity as her literary executor. She types up and annotates page after page of facts that the lawyer is amazed anyone cares to know: The famous writer was born in Lansing, Michigan, the youngest of three children. The famous writer wore size-seven shoes. The famous writer never married, though she was rumored to have carried on long-term affairs with either her editor or his wife or both. Over and over again, he tells the story of how the ashes wound up in his filing cabinet: How the firm's senior partner was the famous writer's attorney. How some arcane clause in her will about the interment of her ashes proved impossible to fulfill. How she sat in the morgue, unclaimed, because there was no one left who wanted her. How her lawyer took pity on her and brought her back to the office, where she has stayed ever since. He styles himself as the successor of a noble duty, defender of the famous writer's honor. He is her champion, her advocate, her savior. He answers every question imaginable on the subject of the famous writer: Has he considered turning her ashes into diamonds? What about stained glass? Is it true he refused to sell her to a Saudi prince? What does he say to claims that the ashes in the urn do not belong to the famous writer at all, that she is in fact alive and well in Panama and publishing romance novels under an assumed name? After fielding all these questions, he begins to feel he must be the world's foremost expert on the famous writer and her ashes.

Sales of the famous writer's books double, and the lawyer receives several offers from publishers to reissue those of her works that have fallen out of print. One publishing house even proposes a limited edition of the famous writer's collected works printed in ink mixed from her ashes, but this the lawyer declines. He is approached about a movie deal for her most famous novel, and another for her life rights, to make a sudsy awards-season biopic. When he asks who will play the lawyer who is contractually obligated to look after her remains, they do not laugh.

Meanwhile, business has never been better. In addition to the appearance fees for all the talk shows and morning programs, there has been an influx of new clients. Many of them don't even have real cases. They simply want to pay his consultation fee for the chance to get a glimpse of the famous writer's ashes, sitting on their shelf in his waiting room.

The lawyer congratulates himself on his success. Everything is turning out better than he could ever have expected when he decided to give that first interview. All his colleagues want to know how he ever came up with the idea to display the famous writer's ashes in the first place. Everyone agrees that he was really on to something. He tells them it's the least he can do to recognize such an underappreciated figure of modern literature.

One day, the lawyer is invited to a roundtable discussion with a popular academic and a noted literary critic. He lies awake the night before, worrying that this will be the day he is exposed as a pretender, that the academic will be waiting to catch him out with some obscure piece of trivia about the famous writer's life. But as soon as the discussion begins, he finds the previous night's anxieties almost comical. Nobody can tell he's reciting the paralegal's talking points by rote. He is the youngest of the three men onstage, and the fittest, and the best dressed. The academic has a stain on his shirt, badly hidden by his tie. Of course he belongs on this stage, with all these people looking up at him. He is the keeper of the famous writer's legacy.

When he gets back to the office, the lawyer tells the paralegal they are both taking the afternoon off in recognition of all their hard work. She says it is no hardship to honor someone she truly admires, and declines his offer of a celebratory drink. "Maybe next time," she says, with a conciliatory air, as if she's letting him down. As if his idea of a good time is wasting top-shelf liquor on another one of her endless monologues of literary trivia. He spends enough time faking an interest in the famous writer as it is.

Two drinks in, he calls the reporter from the arts and leisure section and invites her to dinner—to thank her for the good publicity, he says in his message—but she does not return his call. Instead, he orders some expensive takeout and spends the rest of the night at home, watching reruns of a sitcom starring an actress whose small breasts and sunken clavicles remind him of the reporter's. After a while, he gets tired of peering into the shadows of the actress's low-cut blouse and opens his favorite porn site. He starts with videos of thin, motionless women being fucked on their hands and knees, but soon he finds himself scrolling through videos of men stroking themselves with steel wool and fistfuls of stinging nettles, until, at last, he finds a low-res camera-phone clip of a man rutting against a mound of dirt while the noise of traffic drones in the background, and the lawyer comes blandly inside his shorts. He clears his browser history and clears it again.

Now everyone he meets wants to talk to him about cremation. They introduce themselves at parties, stop him in line at the delicatessen. "Aren't you that lawyer with the ashes?" they say. They look at him with bright, dilated eyes, mouths already half-open, eager to share their own brush with the dead. One woman tells him she carried her nana's ashes with her across seventeen states, until, she admits tearfully, they were lost in a move. His clients, he learns, have had their loved ones made into pencils and fireworks and silicone glaze. One man spends his entire consultation bragging about how he once smoked Jessica Tandy's ashes. A woman comes to see if he can find a loophole in her great-aunt's will, which leaves her a beautiful historic mansion, on the condition that she must mix the old lady's remains into house paint and apply it to her home. She does not, she says, want to live somewhere painted with a dead woman.

The paralegal convinces the lawyer to start looking for additional help so he can focus his attention on the appearances and public-speaking engagements. "Seeking hardworking associate to join small entertainment law firm," the job ad reads. "Must not be offended by presence of human remains." So far, the response has not been stellar.

Late one evening, after another round of subpar interviews for the new associate, the lawyer walks out into the waiting room to find the paralegal standing on a step stool, polishing the urn with a cloth. He stands in the doorway for a while, watching as she buffs the surface of the urn to a high shine. She is talking to it, he realizes, in a whisper so low he cannot hear. But when she turns and wishes him a good night, he decides he must have been mistaken.

It seems that the ashes have infiltrated every aspect of his life. When he walks down the street, he can feel strangers staring at him, as if they are waiting to talk about him as soon as he's out of earshot, and he knows it's the ashes they will discuss. He wakes in the middle of the night, certain the famous writer is standing over him, fixing him with the intense, inscrutable gaze she wears in all her author photos. He hates that sidelong, haughty look she has, the way it seems to suggest she is thinking something he will never be allowed to know. Over and over he dreams he is sinking into a pale, sensual powder.

He tries for a while not to think about the famous writer's ashes. He doesn't appreciate the extent to which they have overtaken his imagination. There was a time when he didn't dream about carnal encounters with human remains. There was a time when he didn't dream at all.

When one of the clerks he knows from the courthouse asks him out to dinner, he feels a rush of relief. At the restaurant, she laughs at his jokes, appears to be impressed by his knowledge of the wine list. They are contemplating dessert when she suggests they go back to her place instead. In the car, he reflects with satisfaction on how well things are going, but by the time they get to her apartment, he isn't much interested in her anymore. The clerk tries to entice him, but he is able to excite himself only by picturing her fragile body crumbling under his grip. He imagines her bones as a pile of dust and shards.

Every day, he sits in his office and considers the urn, just out of sight on its shelf in the waiting room. He likes knowing she's there, always waiting. He thinks almost constantly of fine ash sticking to his slick skin, the rough scrape of porous shards of bone against his tenderest flesh. Any spare moment he doesn't have a client, he's searching for new ways to satisfy his craving—a video of a man shoving his penis into a dish of diatomaceous earth, or another of a woman sinking into quicksand until every inch of her disappears. The look on her face, the supple O of her mouth as she vanishes from sight—he comes furiously, shuddering all over, his guts tangled into searing knots.

The lawyer worries that soon these substitutes will no longer be enough. Of course, he could get rid of the famous writer's ashes before their temptation becomes too much. He could call some museums to inquire about donating human remains. He could take another look at the famous writer's will to see if there's a loophole that would permit him to inter the ashes or scatter them over the sea. He imagines opening a window in one of the elevated trains and letting the ashes sift through his fingers to disperse over the city streets. He could pour the ashes into a plastic bag one night when no one was looking and do anything he wanted with them. No one would have to know.

The paralegal notices the toll his yearning has begun to take on him. She remarks solicitously on the dark circles under his eyes, offering recipes for herbal sleep aids and coordinating with job candidates so he doesn't have to deal with interviews. One evening, she appears in the door to his office and says, "Let me finish filing those for you. You should go home and get some rest." He agrees, and goes home to rut into a dish of cool charcoal ash and sob with unsatisfied longing.

Nothing will ever be enough. The lawyer knows this now, with the dull certainty of a stomachache. He has rubbed himself raw trying to fuck a two-pound bag of crushed oyster shells he bought off the internet, all for nothing. No sensation alone will suffice, no simulacra, because what he wants is not the feel of just any ashes, but of something that was once a woman and now is not. And if he can't have it, he feels sure that he will die.

One quiet Sunday, he packs up his briefcase and heads into work in the late afternoon, when he's sure no one else will be in the office. He locks all the doors and pulls the shades. Gently, he takes the famous writer's ashes down from the shelf and sets the urn on his desk. Then he shoves a chair under the handle of his door, just for good measure.

This is it, he tells himself as he takes off his clothes and folds them neatly on his ergonomic desk chair. He is already powerfully aroused, his nipples tightening when the air conditioning switches on. He stands before his desk in anticipation of his reunion with the famous writer's ashes.

He lifts the lid of the urn, holding his breath so as not to disturb a single particle of her. The urn is empty. Its insides are immaculately clean. In vain he runs his fingers along the bottom of the urn, then touches them to his tongue in the hope of finding one fleeting taste of the writer's ashes, but there's nothing left—nothing but a note, written in the paralegal's careful hand, which reads: "I'm taking her away from you. Don't try to find us. We are in love. You do not deserve her."

Standing before the urn, naked in air that suddenly feels much too cold, he knows he should be thinking back on the choices that have led him to this point, trying to work out how this could have happened right under his nose without his ever noticing. He knows he should be angry or jealous or aggrieved. But all he can think of, beyond the spring of futile, annihilating longing that is welling up inside him, is the two of them together— the paralegal standing on the subway, holding on to a strap with one hand, tenderly cradling a silver box filled with the famous writer's ashes in the crook of her arm, the noise of the train on the tracks like the rhythm of a heartbeat around them—as they are carried farther and farther away.

TO BUFFALO EASTWARD

BY GABRIEL BUMP

So, the sunrise outside Ann Arbor—I figured I'd say something about that. I was in my parked car, reclined all the way, feet pressed against the radio, thinking about falling asleep there, outside that gas station. I was less than halfway to where I was headed when I saw the sun come over the pines, when I decided to keep going, when I decided to stop smoking, after just this last one.

The cigarette bounced out my rolled-down window, caught a breeze, floated into grass sparkled with dew. I had started, miles before the sunrise, to describe things in my head as *sparkled*, *dazzled*, *majestic*, and so on. Water and seagulls underneath the Mackinac Bridge during last night's sunset—that was glitter. I had crossed the bridge; I had decided to stop smoking, after just that last one. That cigarette hit a car's windshield and flew into the straits. In my rearview mirror: sparks and a swearing woman. She passed me on a slight curve, flipped me off, sped onto an exit ramp. I'd expected as much. Once, back home on our major road, a woman threw a hamburger against my window, made me swerve a bit.

There was a bookstore in Ann Arbor. Before another sunset, I stood looking at the novels and short stories and no one asked if I needed help. A person in college-themed sweatpants dropped their stack on my feet. I joked that my feet were made of titanium. The person in college-themed sweatpants laughed and invited me to a party, wrote an address in my phone, smiled after the books were rearranged in their arms. I told them my schedule was tight, which it wasn't, was never.

Outside the bookstore, in my car, I read about this new drug for depression and anxiety. It was a shot for which you had to pay thousands of dollars. I wondered if I needed a shot like that. One of my problems is not understanding my problems. I sat with my therapist and talked about childhood memories. I have problems telling stories. I get on one track and backflip to another, running in the opposite direction. One second I'm pulling a freight train from Kansas City to Las Vegas. The next second I'm in southern

Indiana, headed to Atlanta. I know that's a problem. I wish I understood it. I watched a man in glasses leave the bookstore with a paper bag. I watched the paper bag rip. I laughed hard enough to cough. That was another thing wrong with me: laughing, at first, when someone needed help. I'd laugh before helping. I'd still help. I'd laugh first. Coughing in my car, I wondered if they had shots for whatever was wrong with me. The man didn't want help. He waved me away, grumbled into his fallen books, adjusted his tie, swore with a Nordic-sounding cadence, yelled at a bus for almost breaking his legs.

That was the bookstore in Ann Arbor.

At a liquor store in Ann Arbor, I weighed a plastic bottle of vodka in my hand. I picked up a bigger bottle and held it like an old cat.

In a grocery store parking lot in Ann Arbor, I slept and dreamed that all my pants were back home, folded and forgotten in my drawer. There was loud music in my dream and I was naked, not having a good time, getting yelled at by a disembodied voice.

Outside a house party in Ann Arbor, I counted people on a porch, counted people through the front window, counted people dancing, counted people talking, hugging, drinking, shaking hands.

Outside a house party in Ann Arbor, I pulled away.

I found a motel near the highway, off the southbound side.

Here's my point: that was day two.

I woke up in the darkness. Soon there it was: my life, it seemed, coming over the pines.

Day three would find me pulling into Buffalo around dinnertime.

There was a bookstore in Toledo, the Maumee River, places to sit along its banks, bars with small TVs showing baseball and game shows. Toledo seemed like enough for me. I carried my book and beer to the water, wanted a peaceful moment to watch smoke waft from the industrial parts of town into my lungs. I said something about America's decline to myself, out loud.

"Excuse me?" a jogging man said, slowed down in front of me, blocked my view.

"Nothing," I said. "Talking to myself."

"You can't drink here," the jogging man said, still jogging in place.

"I'm not drinking," I said.

"I'm not stupid," the jogging man said.

"I don't know you," I said.

The jogging man scoffed, continued on his way, glanced over his shoulder, made sure I wasn't following and foaming out of my lips.

Here's how I look: tallish; medium-brown freckles around my nose and eyes, on my ears; a broad nose with a little point, a little hook; strong-chinned; weak-bodied;

soft, thin, broad-shouldered; my nails get too long before I chew them down; my foot arches are too high; without thinking, I walk on my toes; if I'm not mindful, my eyebrows can meld into a single thicket.

I have this ambiguous brown skin. People wonder if I'm Egyptian, Aboriginal, Brazilian, Mexican, Dominican, half of this, a quarter of that.

I have this long hair that grows up and out in curled waves. People don't know what to make of it. In middle school, this classmate would pull at my hair, try to yank strands out, hold my curls up to the light.

When I was little, people thought my mother was my nanny. My mother was a dean at Upper Peninsula State College. She taught classes on economics, gave lectures on employee happiness. She wrote a book about suicide rates in Silicon Valley. She told me to find pleasure in work, keep an eye on your heart and soul. She grew up in the projects in Chicago, would always tell me how she grew up in the projects and could whoop my ass. Once, we tried to visit her childhood home in Chicago. We parked our car outside a chain-link fence with no buildings behind it. It was the largest empty lot I had ever seen. The city had blown up my mother's childhood home. They were going to build condos and offices, hair salons and organic grocery stores. Parked outside that chain-link fence, my mother cried about history. All her family was dead and buried in modest graves in Chicago, Harlem, Oklahoma City, and Georgia. When she felt like it, my mother could grow an Afro with gray streaks blaring from her temples.

Before I left, my mother gave me an industrial wrench for protection, in case my car broke down in Ohio and some local boys wanted to take advantage.

My father asked me to procure sports memorabilia, bring it back at Christmas, wrap it up, make it nice. In our kitchen, my father had a coffee mug from every NHL team, most MLB teams, half of the NBA, some NFL. He wrote a book about traveling to professional sports arenas around America. He wanted to write a screenplay about himself and sell it to Hollywood.

For years, my father reported on high school sports for our local newspaper. Then, when the newspaper folded, he wrote a sports column for a local website. Then, after the town turned Republican, he started folding political jokes into his analysis, speaking truth to power, rambling on about the declining American mystique, eroding values. He resigned after someone mailed a dead rat to our house. We moved at night. That was a few years ago. We all cried in my mother's car.

I majored in European history, worked at UPSC's library, lived at home, hung around people and places I had always known.

I finished my beer on the Maumee. I found a route to

Cleveland that took me along Lake Erie at a slow pace, through lowlands and forests.

There was a bookstore in Cleveland. There were stacks so tall you needed a ladder to reach the top. I asked a man with a ponytail if he could help with those Raymond Carver collections up there. He was a carpenter, not a librarian, he told me as much, hand on his hip, other hand holding Joyce and Morrison. He told me to climb the ladder myself, it wasn't that high, I wasn't that small.

When I came down, the man asked me to drink with him. He knew a spot next door, with TVs and boiled hot dogs—Cleveland against Minneapolis, which I knew before he told me. I looked at my wrist, forgot I'd left my watch back home with Pidge, as a way for her to remember me.

Pidge had kissed me before I left Michigan, on a gravel road, under a moon-draped evergreen, between two small lakes.

Whenever I texted Pidge on the road, I would think about turning around and driving back, which Pidge didn't want, because Pidge has a fiancé. I would tell her about driving back. She'd call me "stupid" and "emotional."

One night back home, I stood outside my parked car, leaned against my hood, keeping track of an owl hooting its way across the lakes. Pidge was supposed to meet me at midnight. We were supposed to drive down to Kenosha, get an apartment, get two kittens, work from home, write books, cook global cuisines. Pidge was supposed to leave her fiancé. I waited until three in the morning. When she came in to work the next day, carrying her coffee and hand-made satchel, I asked her to lunch. She declined with a thank-you. When I saw her after work, walking across the quad, I asked if I could call her later that night. She held my hands and apologized, said I couldn't, sorry.

"Huh?" the carpenter asked.

"Nothing," I said. "Talking to myself."

"Do you need a drink?" the carpenter asked. "I need a drink."

"I need to get to Buffalo," I said.

"That's close," the carpenter said.

He ordered two Miller Lites for himself, opened both, sipped both, opened his Joyce, laid it out between his arms, kept it open with his elbows. I wanted vodka. I wanted to know how this carpenter managed all these things at once. I imagined his works as solid—bookcases and skyscrapers, barns and avant-garde chairs. Minneapolis hit a home run into shallow left field. I ordered a Miller Lite. The carpenter flicked up one elbow, took a sip, and turned the page.

I waited for the carpenter to tell me something. Two women walked in falling over, held each other up, almost didn't make it to the bar, winked at us, blew us kisses, fell over laughing. I looked up at the screen, watched a batter get hit on the foot by a fastball. I figured I could leave at any moment and no one would notice. I worked through my next steps.

First, make it out of Cleveland alive.

Second, get some lunch on the way to Buffalo.

Third, call Flip when I got close.

Fourth, live in Buffalo.

First, I had to finish my beer.

"What's he reading?" the two women asked at the same time now, standing behind me.

"Joyce," I said. "I think."

"*Dubliners*!" one woman said.

"*Finnegans Wake*!" the other woman said.

I tried to find a difference between their faces, their hair, their dark eyes made darker by the lightless bar. Both had black hair straightened flat, small eyes close to their noses.

The carpenter drained one can, then another. He turned his head away and belched into his armpit.

"*Ulysses*," the carpenter said, closed the book, showed them the cover.

"Yes!" one woman yelled.

"I said yes!" the other woman yelled.

"I will yes!" one woman yelled.

Two outs into the third inning, the women introduced themselves. My eyes had adjusted to the darkness. Now I could see unique lines and blemishes on their cheeks and necks. Whenever they laughed, I noticed the different ways their teeth zagged. They wore matching blue lipstick. Their touches on my shoulder were different weights, whenever the carpenter made a joke about literature and the women couldn't hold firm on their feet, needed me to keep them up. We had arranged ourselves in a small circle. The carpenter and I had our backs to the game. We ordered more beer. We went around and said our names.

"Sancho," the carpenter said. "Sancho Panza."

"And I'm Daisy Buchanan," one woman said, laughing, heavy hand on my shoulder.

"I'm Jordan Fucking Baker," the other woman said, emptying a beer can into her face.

"What about our real names?" I asked.

"I'm Daisy Buchanan," Daisy Buchanan said. "I'm alone and boring."

"That's unfair," Jordan Baker said. "That's a shallow interpretation."

"I'm Daisy Buchanan," Daisy Buchanan said. "I'll steal your man. I'll steal your car."

"I'm Sancho Panza," Sancho Panza said. "I work for an idiot, a monster, a liar."

"Who are you?" Jordan Baker asked me, leaned forward in her stool, winked.

I tried to remember all the books I loved, all the characters I couldn't forget. I imagined myself back home, years ago, a child, kneeling in my mother's small library, thumbing through the hardcover and paperback rows. I heard my mother's feet come up the stairs, kick at the door, soft, nice. I heard my mother telling me to get out with my grease-stained fingers, my mud-stained shoes. I remember the book I had hidden in my shirt when she pushed me out, locked the door.

"I'm Invisible," I said. "I'm the Invisible Man."

"The lights!" Daisy Buchanan yelled.

We emptied our beers, ordered more, asked for a plate of hot dogs with mustard slathered on the buns.

During the seventh-inning stretch, Jordan Baker explained how love evaporates.

"It's like this friendship," Jordan Baker said. "After a while, if it's not going to work, you start to hate each other. You get annoyed every time they want to dance with you at a party. You hear them crying in the bathroom after another yelling match, and you get annoyed because they're crying and you have to make them feel better, tell them you're sorry. You hate them. Still, you're friends, best friends, because if you spend that much time with someone, those many years, you have to care about them, even if you hate them, even if you can't eat at the same time as them because they chew with their mouths open and smack their lips like they've always done. Still, one day you decide to leave. Still, it hurts. Even if you hate them, it hurts."

I expected Jordan Baker to slow down, stop talking. She didn't stop. Instead, I excused myself, waddled to the bathroom, wiped my eyes, told myself not to cry in front of strangers.

I splashed hard, cold water on my face, slapped my cheeks, told myself I wasn't going to die alone.

Pidge isn't why I left home. Pidge didn't force me to Buffalo. Still, I would've liked Pidge to come with me. I thought we'd have fun driving with the windows down, trying out new lives.

Pidge's fiancé teaches in the engineering department. He studies ice fishing and climate change. Pidge has a picture of him on her office desk. He's shirtless on a mountain, smiling, trying to cover his belly fat with his slim arms. He's a nice-looking guy. His students nominate him for teaching awards. Once, he answered when I called Pidge's cell phone. She was taking a nap. He asked to take a message. I told him Pidge had overdue books and the fines were starting to get serious. He apologized. I apologized. He hung up. I held the phone to my face.

Pidge would leave me notes on her library cards. They would say things like "You're my primary source" and "Check me out any day."

Once, Pidge kissed me in the Medieval Medicine section.

When I got back, it was Daisy Buchanan's turn.

"It's like waking up from a nightmare," Daisy Buchanan

said. "It's three in the morning, you're sweating. Your nightmares were about falling into a canyon, flying into the sun, whatever. You're up and looking around, gasping for air, all this sweat on your back and face. And then you hear this voice telling you it's okay. It was just a nightmare, it's okay. This voice is close to your face, tickling your ear. It's telling you to go back to sleep. It's okay. It's just a nightmare. And calm comes over you like a cold snap."

"I've heard that voice," Sancho Panza said.

"Then one morning," Daisy Buchanan continued, "you forget your lunch at home. You drive back from work. You open the door. And that calming voice is naked in your kitchen, making pancakes with your naked next-door neighbor."

At the top of the ninth inning, Minneapolis had the tying run on first base, with some power at the plate. Sancho Panza crushed a beer can flat between his palms. He flung the disk at a trash can fifteen feet away. He missed; we booed; he went out for a cigarette; we followed. Jordan Baker sat on a fire hydrant, rubbed her face, stamped a fallen branch to pieces.

"We need an adventure," Daisy Buchanan said.

"We could go to the harbor," Sancho Panza said.

"What's at the harbor?" I asked.

"Water," Sancho Panza said. "A lake. Waves."

"I've seen enough lakes," I said. "I'm sick of water."

"Sometimes," Jordan Baker said, "I feel like floating until I sink."

"No water," Daisy Buchanan said. "Let's climb something."

"I know roofs," Sancho Panza said. "I have keys and back doors."

"Once," Jordan Baker said, "in high school, I watched a woman ride a motorcycle into a pool. I bet that's happening somewhere tonight."

"You're right," Sancho Panza said. "We need transportation."

We emptied the junk from my backseat, mixed it with the mess in my trunk—books, clothes, chips bags, candy wrappers: my life laid bare for them to inspect and handle. We found a liquor store up the road, bought pints of flavored schnapps. We listened to country music. We tried to guess the words to songs we hadn't heard before, wouldn't hear again. We missed a turn. We didn't talk about our unpaid tab at the bar. We didn't talk about one another. There was nothing to know. In my front seat, Jordan Baker tapped on the glass, told us life was a series of fishbowls. Behind me, Daisy Buchanan and Sancho Panza rubbed at each other, made kissing noises.

"Here!" Sancho Panza yelled. "Turn! Park!"

We parked and looked up at an office building—a three-story structure made of windows and thick black metal strips.

"There are people," I said, pointing at workers in suits and dresses, carrying briefcases, trudging around, slumping into cars.

"Nine-to-five," Daisy Buchanan said. "I couldn't do it."

"They sell metal pipes," Sancho Panza said. "Some of them sell potato chips, I think."

"How do you know?" I asked.

"This is mine," Sancho Panza said.

"You own this building?" I asked.

"Other buildings too," Sancho Panza said. "A pizza place, that bar, that bookstore."

"You have an empire," Daisy Buchanan said.

"I am benevolent," Sancho Panza said. "I am cruel only when the hour demands it."

Sancho Panza had a key to a back door. He challenged us to race up a metal stairway. We passed a man smoking a cigar and crying into his cell phone. We passed a well-dressed couple laughing and pressing into each other. We exited onto a wide roof, where a woman in a skirt was juggling three empty beer bottles. Startled, she fumbled her trick, disappeared into another doorway, another staircase.

Here, Sancho Panza reached into his pocket and materialized four pills, each a different brilliant color. Now someone commented on the view, how flat and boring it appeared, a repeated system of low buildings and mediocre trees. Now we took the pills.

That wasn't the first time I had taken pills from a stranger's pocket. In high school, around a campfire, on a small, abandoned island, a girl's older boyfriend asked if we wanted to feel the universe against our minds. "Sure," we said, bored, a little drunk, smiling at one another through the low flames. That island was abandoned in a bureaucratic sense. Somewhere, down an untraceable line, someone had stopped paying taxes on the land; somewhere, a bank sent a hollow person to put up foreclosure signs on the island's banks. We had never known the delinquent landowner.

There was a home yards away from the campfire. There was another up from the dock, a short hike uphill. Around the campfire, we took the pills and went into the closer house. Whenever we were bored and a little drunk, sick of staring at fire and embers, talking about fishing and car crashes on the hairpin turn near town, we'd stand up and walk into the home. Yes, the home was abandoned in the bureaucratic sense. Most nights and days, no one walked around in there, picking things up, putting things down, calling through doors and walls, walking carefully up the stairs. Still, a mattress sat, soiled and deflated, in the living room. Words spray-painted on the walls almost covered all the exposed wood beams. This was an abandoned house on a small island: everything you'd imagine. Our pills kicked in, we wrestled into a big pile in the second-floor bedroom. Later, we all linked arms and looked out a broken window onto our lakes. The late-night stillness heightened our experience, as if the water was one big mirror that could swallow our souls, the ghosts inside us. We waited for sunrise in the living room, standing in a line, arm in arm, looking at the dirt- and dust-covered floor, looking. The girl's older boyfriend saw a muskrat playing in the sink. No one else saw it; no one else looked. Instead, we saw snow falling, soft flurries taking long, curved routes to the water and dirt. We stayed like that until the flurries turned into a solid white sheet, cascading down on us. The pills wore off when it was too late. Sober, in the morning light, we had to shovel snow from our boats before they sank. We had to think of excuses for our parents. The girl's older boyfriend panicked, started pacing around and talking about cops coming on boats and helicopters and submarines. He started telling us about microphones in tree trunks, cameras in vermin. That muskrat! He yelled about that muskrat until we subdued him in well-formed football tackles from multiple angles. We put our hands over his mouth. We finished shoveling our boats after he went back to sleep. We left him there. Once, I saw him pushing carts around the grocery store. I saw him on a tractor riding through town. I saw him, from a bridge, running across a frozen river.

Back on the roof, in Cleveland, Sancho Panza wanted to know if the pills were working—could we feel ourselves turning inside out, exploding like a flower?

"I could wake up in Egypt," Jordan Baker said.

"What difference would it make?" Daisy Buchanan asked.

"I'd have all the sand I could want," Jordan Baker said.

"There's sand in Ohio!" Daisy Buchanan said.

"Not the same," Jordan Baker said, sat on the ground. "It's just not the same."

I found myself yards away, walking in a circle, counting my revolutions.

I found myself running into Sancho Panza, knocking him over.

Sancho Panza grabbed my ankles, begged me not to let him drown.

I had my hands on Sancho Panza's collar when I noticed the sky, swirling and wavering, preparing to rupture. Out there in the distance, toward downtown, the sky sucked up tall buildings.

"It's coming for us," I said.

Sancho Panza had stopped swinging at my throat and screaming. He went limp, took deep breaths, turned an ear to the roof, coughed, and spit up thick brown mucus.

"They're working," Sancho Panza said. "I think they're working."

Daisy Buchanan and Jordan Baker appeared, flanked me, trained their large pupils on my cheeks.

"Look," I told them, "this sky is bad business."

They jerked their heads upward, gaped at moving clouds.

"Don't you see it?" Daisy Buchanan asked.

"Of course," Jordan Baker said. "It's right there. Of course."

"My school bus," Daisy Buchanan said. "Right there. I'm right there waving for help."

"That's my submarine," Jordan Baker said. "Those are my specimens."

I couldn't explain how their eyes and minds were playing tricks. There wasn't a school bus; there wasn't a submarine. Above our heads, there weren't roads or seas or highways or rivers. It was all teeth and tongues.

Sancho Panza, reanimated, grabbed my leg, tried to climb up.

"My uncle," Sancho Panza said, drooled. "There was Easter breakfast at his farmhouse."

"I didn't finish my homework," Daisy Buchanan said. "Why can't I finish anything?"

"At these depths," Jordan Baker said, "we know more about the moon."

"You don't see it," I said. "You'll never see it."

"There's my daughter," Daisy Buchanan said, pointed behind us without looking. "Just like me: late and unprepared. And that face. Just like mine. Look how she hates it. Look how she can't stand it."

"Sunlight doesn't penetrate," Jordan Baker said. "Not this deep. Not under this pressure. It's all scientific, these things I don't understand. There's my power glowing in the abyss, protected by Paleolithic megasharks. It's all academic. It's all too scientific for me to understand."

"What?" I asked.

"Nothing," Jordan Baker said. "What did I say?"

"Uncle," Sancho Panza said, "why didn't you save me any coffee cake?"

We spent hours like that: talking and not understanding one another's eyes. At some point we left the roof, went to a lower floor, used Sancho Panza's master key to open offices and inspect other people's lives. We took framed family photos off desks, held them, and cried. We found liquor bottles in bottom drawers, took long sips. We found charts and graphs and memos; we felt connected to important happenings. In a large office, we found a list of underperforming employees. In a small office, we found a vision board with a spaceship and tiny glow-in-the-dark stars.

We finished in a conference room. Somewhere along the way, Jordan Baker had assembled a collection of stolen blankets. We all said goodnight. We kissed one another's hands. We pulled the blankets over our heads and blocked the rising sun. Curled against these whacked-out strangers, I felt a unique warmth, one I hadn't known before. I felt clear and directed, anchored. I had found peace. Here, I belonged.

I closed my eyes.

Instead of sleeping, I saw Pidge sliding across a frozen lake in her purple boots, twirling, extending her arms, teasing me, saying I couldn't keep up. Under her winter cap, her blond hair stiff against her neck. Her small frame puffed by her jacket and snow pants. Her nose crooked from a hockey fight, still black-and-blue. Her chipped teeth jagged in her smile. Brown eyes, almost black. She was sliding toward me now, getting smaller, getting faster.

That was Pidge during a break in a blizzard. Her fiancé wasn't her fiancé yet. Her fiancé was her boyfriend, out of town and stuck there because the blizzard was everywhere in the upper Midwest. We had brought bags of frozen burritos and beer to Pidge's apartment and holed up with movies and video games. Pidge, during her hockey game, had called an opposing player unkind names. They'd settled it with fists to the face and stomach. They'd both lost, busted up parts of their bodies and pride. I'd offered to help Pidge convalesce.

During a break in the blizzard, we bundled up and went for the lake.

Pidge sliding toward me, kicking up snow and ice, busting forth in a beautiful mist.

Pidge laughing at my unsteady feet, my wobbling.

Pidge confused—how could I not skate? Growing up around all this frozen water. How could I not skate?

Pidge slowing down, putting her heels down, kicking snow onto my legs.

Pidge spearing me to the ground.

Us cold on our backs.

Me asking if she was okay, putting my arms around her.

Pidge laughing, laughing, laughing, laughing.

Me slipping as I stood up.

Pidge staying down there, rolling around, laughing still.

I awoke to a man screaming, standing in the conference room doorway, spilling his coffee down his shirt.

Sancho Panza told me to run. He cupped my cheek with his hand. He'd handle it. Fly. Take your life. Jordan Baker and Daisy Buchanan were already gone. I could see their hair strands tangled in their blankets. I ran past the screaming man, ducked into a stairwell.

On my way down, I passed a man and a woman talking about running away, starting a new life, antiquing, scoring big at an auction, building a house in a tree.

On my driver's-side window, a note was written in blue lipstick. It read: "Invisible Man, make it where you're going."

SUPPLY AND DEMAND

BY ANJALI SACHDEVA

Liam rings the bell outside my door and waits respectfully for me to answer, though I can see the shadows of his feet shifting with impatience. I pull on a robe, open the curtains to let in a little light, go to the door, and slide back the bar to unlock it. It's early for me but late, I know, for him. He'll have been up since sunrise, answering all the questions fifty men can generate overnight. How much water is in the cisterns? How much chicken and rabbit meat is in the smokehouse? Which cabins need to be repaired, and who will do it, and when? I don't know whether he's here for his ration or for a favor or whether one of the kids is in trouble, but it doesn't really matter. Our camp is stable and peaceful, thanks to him, and I never keep him waiting if I can help it.

When he sees me he smiles, his usual smile that means he's preoccupied with something else.

"What can I do for you?" I ask.

He says that Grayson's been feeling low, and it would sure mean a lot to him if he could get a little extra, that then maybe he'd get back to doing the repairs he's supposed to be doing on the wagons, and that would benefit everyone. Says he knows I'm busy and he doesn't like to interfere, but anyway he brought me this pillow, if I'd like it, just in recognition. A whole conversation where I never open my mouth, because I don't have to. It's a one-sided negotiation and he knows it. He has more power than any man here, but if I accept it'll be because I'm feeling generous. I take the pillow from him and squeeze it against my chest. It's a good one, goose down, hours and hours of labor taken to spin the thread, weave the fabric, collect the feathers. And it's mine no matter how I answer him.

"Tell him he can come after sunset," I say. I'm always impatient in the heat. "Actually, I'll tell him myself."

"Thank you," he says, and he nods and pulls the door shut and leaves me to the rest of my day.

Before Grayson, I'll sleep with five other men today. A twenty-minute ration for each, thirty minutes in between. I could space it out more and sometimes I do, but there's no one in the rotation today who I especially like, and sometimes I just want to get on with my day. To have time to linger over my lunch or take a walk in the pinewood with the kids, or daydream, or lend a hand with someone else's project.

Today I'm working on a pair of boots for Prima, my eldest daughter, recently returned from a year spent living in the city. I knew early on in my life in camp that I'd need something to keep me busy, a hobby, and don't ask me why I decided to learn shoemaking, other than that we had a book about it. Lots of books like that around here. No *Good Housekeeping* or romance novels, but everything you ever wanted to know about handicrafts and pioneer times. God forbid anyone should get hold of a microwave or a circular saw, since they might find some way to turn it into a weapon, and if living without technology makes everything a little more difficult, well, it's all for the best, in the long run. We're supposed to act like we've just been returned to some previous way of living and can slot in like little pegs. Complete bullshit, but I guess it's not all wrong. I make good boots.

In the few years that I dated—my late teens, a world ago—the guys I went out with usually showed up late. They'd be sweaty or dirty, T-shirts stretched at the collar. Often they hardly seemed to remember my name, though they'd come up to me at a restaurant or at school saying, "Hey, beautiful, can I get your number?" One guy showed up with another girl's lipstick on his neck. One tried to feel me up in a booth at the back of a Panera. Once, a guy propositioned me from the open window of his car, said, "Get in, we'll just go to my place, why waste time talking?"

Of course, not all of them were like this. Some were decent guys who took the trouble to put on button-ups and slacks, who smiled and made an effort and just never called me back. I wasn't what you'd call a catch back then. I was homely and I knew it. The smart thing to do would have been to cultivate something to make up for my looks— some talent, some knowledge or sweetness. But I was too pissed. I thought the world owed me an apology and I made sure everyone knew it. *Common.* That was really the word for me.

But we were all common back then, even the 10s. I used to hate men because they didn't show me any love. Because they looked right through me as if I didn't matter. Well, I didn't. No more than the next woman, and the next, and the next.

When I was a little girl I loved books about unicorns. I used to dream about finding one in the half acre of scrub pine behind my elementary school; about how I would become special just by standing in the soft white light of its horn.

But imagine a world full of unicorns. Unicorns everywhere. Unicorns in the streets, in the parks, in the grocery store. Pale gold or silvery or sparkling like diamonds, moving through rush hour traffic with the grace of butterflies. It wouldn't matter how beautiful they were. You wouldn't see them anymore. They'd be the same as pigeons or stray cats. You wouldn't stop and stare as they passed. If anything, you'd probably start killing them off. That was women, for a millennium or two. Plenty of us. More than they needed. Common as dirt, and they treated us accordingly.

After rations I go to the mess hall for something to eat. My plate sits on the table, piled high with the best cuts of meat, some fruit, a square of cornbread as big as my hand. Even when supplies are running low, no one touches my food.

Apollo comes in while I'm eating, with Lucas, my youngest, on his hip. "He was asking for you," Apollo says, but he bounces and plays with him until I finish eating, until I dust the crumbs from my hands and hold them out for my baby boy. Lucas throws himself into my arms, leans his head against me, and gabbles a long string of words that I can almost make out.

"Where are the rest of them?" I ask.

"Braden and Lissa are in the nursery with Mateo. Haven't seen anyone else since breakfast. Well, except Prima said she was going to take a nap." My look must say it all because he shrugs and says, "Teenagers need a lot of sleep."

Ever since Prima got back from the city, she's been belligerent and distant. The city year is required for all girls who grow up in the camps. We have to give them the choice, the city women say, though I don't see them sending their daughters out here, to give their precious two-mother girls a glimpse of what they're missing. Being conceived in a lab from two eggs doesn't make you perfect, and being a camp girl with a mother *and* a father doesn't make you dirt, but you'd never know it from the way they talk about us in town. I'd heard, from women in other camps who had older girls, that it was hell when their daughters returned. They're hyped up on city life: technology, entertainment, food you don't have to kill or grow yourself. "Sisterhood," too, all the propaganda they've been fed, the friends they've made in their year away. Even just the novelty of it: women everywhere and not a man in sight, an almost-total reversal of what they've known all their lives. Of course, the girls who realize they're attracted to women usually don't come back at all. But as much as the city dwellers like to think they're living in paradise, most of our girls seem to disagree. It takes them a few months to get their heads on straight when they come home, but when they do they're better for it. Maybe we should thank the city for that.

*   *   *

When Grayson comes to my cabin that night, he rings the bell and waits, looking at the ground. I open the door and he silently hands me a clay jar with a piece of honeycomb in it. He is a quiet man, almost twenty years older than me, gray at the temples. Not much for conversation, and awkward in bed, but he can fix anything that breaks around here, his hands are strong, and he has the patience to follow bees back to their hive and the fearless calm to help himself to the honey. I welcome him inside, set the jar on the bedside table, undress him and myself. When he reaches out to touch me, I can see that his hands have been scrubbed until they are pink; I smell the thyme he has rubbed on them to cover the stink of wood stain. So much work to make himself acceptable to me. It counts, it all counts, more than a handsome face or even a sweet word. I push him down onto the bed, climb on top of him, do my best to make him feel desirable for this short space of time. Before I send him home, we eat the honeycomb together.

When I first arrived in camp I was twenty-two. I'd gone through a three-week training before I left the city, which was really three weeks of various instructors trying to talk me out of leaving. There were the soft and grandmotherly types, saying, "Honey, make sure this is what you really want." Drill-sergeant types, who never said the words *whore* or *gender traitor* but made you feel those words all the time. The same women who had no problems visiting the men who worked in brothels just outside the city.

A lot of women quit the training, went back to the city, and figured out some other way to live. I was one of the few who didn't. It wasn't that I was so devoted; I didn't think being a camp wife was my calling or anything. I was just stubborn. I knew what they were up to and I'd never liked being told what to do. And I was sick to death of Sisterhood. All the men being sent away hadn't made me feel any better about myself; it just made me feel as if I'd missed my chance for redemption.

I arrived at the camp on horseback, my arms wrapped around a military policewoman's waist as she guided the horse through the gates. I had never ridden a horse before. I had never been camping. I felt as if I was in some weird theme park, even though the training was supposed to prepare me for this. Everything was new but somehow shabby, the logs of the cabins beaded with sap, the air saturated with a mixture of anger and desire and panic. The MPs never took their hands off their guns, and the one I rode behind reminded me that I could leave anytime I wanted to, that I didn't have to stay even one minute, and that they would much rather escort me back to the city than leave me here. I might have gone, too, but Liam offered his hand to help me down from the horse, stood next to me as I looked at the men.

It had been a while since I had seen that many men in one place. They had been transferred to the camps a couple of months before my arrival, but you'd have thought it had been years, the way they looked so hungry and grim, gathered in the square. They shifted on their feet and stared at me. Liam called for their attention. He was new to being a leader back then, but so sure of himself, so handsome, the kind of man who would have looked right through me in the old world. He waited until every man in the crowd had met his eyes, and said, "If you scare her off, no one else is coming. So leave her alone until she's ready, for all of our sakes." There was some grumbling, but he ignored it. He smiled like he was addressing a group of shareholders instead of a bunch of men facing a lifetime of quarantine, like he couldn't see the haunted looks on their faces.

That night they had a party for me in the mess hall. They had decorated it, but everything looked rough. Sure, a few of them did woodwork or painted as a hobby, maybe there was a plumber or an electrician in there somewhere, but most of them had been programmers, or bank tellers, or servers, or PR managers. A couple years before landing here, they'd all been part of an economy that ran on dollars, not deer pelts and horse tack, and after that they'd been shuffled through a series of "reeducation programs" and detention centers, none of which had helped prepare them for camp life in any practical way. Even the ones who were good cooks weren't used to stewing rabbit on a woodstove—who was, back then? I couldn't have done any better. And it didn't matter. I don't remember what anything tasted like. I remember only how they looked at me. How the sight of me softened their faces, or filled their eyes with desire, as if there was one good thing left in this awful cheat of a world that had been forced on them, and it was me.

The next day I seek out Prima myself, find her currying the horses in the stables. She has always been good with animals, ever since she was a little girl. Because she was my first, I spent more time with her than I have with her siblings, followed her as she chased rabbits across the fields and coaxed squirrels to take corn from her hand. Now her hair is pulled back in a stiff braid and she stands on her tiptoes to reach the middle of the horse's back. I marvel again at how much she's changed in her year away. All her baby fat is gone, leaving behind muscle and curves and a constant frown. I pick up a brush and join her, but soon she takes it from my hand and says, "Not like that."

"What's wrong with the way I'm doing it?"

"You have to put some muscle into it. They're not delicate." She demonstrates with her brush and hands mine back, but as soon as I start again she rolls her eyes.

I drop the brush back into the tack bucket. "Forget it. I'm going to do rations."

"'Going to do rations.' Right."

"What's that supposed to mean?"

"Why don't you just call it what it is?"

"And what is it?"

"You're just… an animal. Breeding stock."

I take a deep breath. "Lucky for you," I say, "or you wouldn't be here."

My work is not a secret between us. We've talked about it since she was old enough to understand. We've had to. In three years, she'll choose her own camp to go to, a whole new group of men to worship and care for her, and she'll have her own rations to deal with. Someday, sooner than I'd like to admit, I'll retire and be replaced by someone else's daughter. I've known this for years. But the contempt I see in her face catches me off guard. To my men I am always beautiful, but the ugliness I feel under Prima's stare rings some old bell inside my chest, a feeling I once knew too well. My voice is rough when I manage to speak. "And it's not just about breeding," I say. "Those are my men. Those are your fathers. We all do our part." I walk away, breathing hard past the tightness in my throat.

Halfway across the yard I run into Apollo, leading Braden by the hand while Lucas toddles ahead of them. Apollo takes one look at me and says, "What's wrong?"

"Nothing," I say, but I gesture vaguely back at the stables, where Prima still stands grooming the horses.

"Let me talk to her."

If anyone has a chance of digging her out of her dark mood, it's him. Back in my early days in camp, I never paid Apollo much attention. I was young, and I liked the men who were more exciting: Liam for his power; Elijah for his good looks; Mateo because he could make me laugh. But after Prima was born, that changed. Apollo spent hours making toys for her, and it didn't take me long to figure out he wasn't doing it to gain my favor. It was for her, just for her, to see the joy on her face when he handed her some new bauble. He would put her in a cradleboard and take her with him everywhere. He weathered her tantrums and moods with a stoicism I could never manage. The odds were against her being his child, biologically, but he didn't seem to care. It made me softer toward him. It made him one of my favorites.

"I'll take these two," I say, and I scoop Lucas onto one hip and Braden onto the other and walk off toward the nursery, where I can bury myself in their childish sweetness for as long as it lasts.

*　　*　　*

Later, Prima finds me and says, "Will you come for a walk with me?" From her, this is an apology. She's been stubborn since she was a baby, when she'd scream as soon as anyone tried to set her down, going from a dead sleep to a squall as soon as you laid her in the crib. If it had been anyone other than my child, I'd have made them beg my pardon on their knees for talking to me the way she did, but now I nod my head grudgingly and go. We walk into the cool of the woods, where the wind sweeps through the boughs of the pine trees like a constant whisper. As soon as we leave the camp behind I can see Prima start to relax; she's always calmer here. At the creek we sit on a broad rock and put our feet in the water. The stone is warm from the sun but the current is chilled by approaching autumn. Prima combs her fingers through the water, picks up a pebble.

"Do you remember when you first came to live here?" she says.

"Of course. I'm not *that* old."

"What was it like?"

I tell her about my arrival, the party. About the first winters, when we'd all crowd into the mess hall to sleep because it cut the cold to have so many bodies in one place. About all the things from the city I used to miss, and what it felt like to stop missing them. She listens, but she's preoccupied, rolling a question around in her mouth until she's finally ready to stumble through it.

"In the city they said that men... Did anyone... Does anyone ever try to... to force you to..." She stops talking again.

"One time," I say. "Early on."

"Who?" she says, and I can see her anxiety as she thinks of all the men she knows, all her possible fathers.

"A man named Cole. Liam traded him to another camp."

"What happened?"

"He came to my room late, in the middle of the night. I didn't think much, back then, about whether to open the door or not. Once he was inside, I tried to tell him to go, but he wouldn't listen; he pushed me down on my bed and kept trying to cover my mouth. Someone heard me screaming. Next thing I knew there was banging on the door and Cole was dumb enough to open it. Liam was there, and five or six men with him.

"I had never seen him look so panicked. Cole could see it too. He said, 'It's no big deal, she's just excited.'

"Liam looked at me, and I tried to say, *No, it wasn't like that*, but I was crying so hard, I couldn't speak.

"'We've already heard your side of it, don't worry,' Liam said. He pulled us both outside and the rest of the men pinned Cole down in the dirt with his arms outstretched. Someone handed Liam a hammer and he held it out to me and said, 'Do you want to do it?'"

"Do what?" says Prima.

"That's what I said. Liam just said, 'Don't worry,' again. He beat Cole's hand with the hammer until it was crushed. Then he put his arm around me and walked me away. Cole was screaming like an animal, but Liam didn't even glance back; he just watched me. He said, 'We'll call the medevac. You tell them a horse stepped on him. Can you do that?'"

"You lied to the MPs?" Prima says.

"It wasn't anyone else's fault but Cole's. Why have everyone punished? Liam promised me it would never happen again, and it hasn't. And it won't happen to you, either."

Prima is silent for a long moment, looking out at the water, and just when I'm about to ask her what she's thinking she says, "They were trying to scare me. They made it sound like it happened all the time, like men raped women and no one did anything about it." Her face is painted with the anger and scorn particular to those young enough to believe in a world of easy dichotomies: true or untrue, and nothing in between. And what is it in me—what fear, what jealousy—that keeps me from correcting her, from saying, *It used to be true.*

She moves closer to me. "They talk about going to the camps like they're talking about someone dying, or else they laugh about them like it's some big joke."

"They're ignorant," I say. "And they want to be. They don't want to believe we can be a family out here too. They don't understand what we're doing."

"Right," she says quietly, "right." She lays her head on my shoulder and we both breathe the smell of the river and retreat into our own thoughts.

After that, things get easier. Prima seems more settled, she works harder, she is kinder to her brothers and sisters, to the men, to me. If she sometimes seems lost in her own thoughts, that's her right. Sometimes she will sidle up to me and whisper some memory of her city days in my ear, and if it's something new since my time, I'll ask her to describe it to me. It's like a secret the two of us share, the peculiarities of this other place, and I'm too selfish to remind her that every grown man she knows once lived there, too, could partake in these same confidences.

Then late one night she knocks on my door. Before I even open it, I know it's her; the men always use the bell.

"Can I come in?" she says.

"For a little while," I tell her. Truthfully, I don't want to talk right now, but she looks so anxious that I can't say no.

"I wanted to give you something," she says. She hands me a small box. The box itself is miraculous, smooth white cardboard that I could crush with my hands. I haven't seen cardboard in decades. We make paper, but it's a chore, time-consuming; we don't make much of it and certainly not enough to waste on things like this. I run my fingers across the surface. Inside is a puff of cotton, and pinned through that a pair of earrings. Some old part of me appraises them and sees them for what they are: gold plating and strings of glittering cut glass. In my childhood I could have bought them at any mall. But the main part of me doesn't care. They are wonders, among the class of things lost to us out here in the hinterland. I will not see anything so fine in my life again, and when I wear them the men will admire them and touch them reverently, like the relics they are.

"They're beautiful," I say.

She smiles. "I chose them."

"I'm surprised they let you bring them back here." As soon as I say this her smile falters. She sits back from the light of the candle on the bedside table. I wait for her to speak until I can't take the tension, and then I gently lift her chin. "Whatever you want to say, just say it."

"I'm going back," she says.

As soon as she says it I see that I should have known. It seems painfully obvious. The way she talks about the city, like someone describing their beloved. What did I think— that she loved us too much to go? That she could appreciate this life the way I do? I start to ask her why and stop. I don't know if I can bear her answer. Instead I say, "When?"

"Tomorrow. I know I should have told you sooner. I tried. I just kept thinking that if I waited long enough I would change my mind, and then there would be nothing to tell."

Before I can respond the bell rings outside, and when I don't answer it rings again. "Go away," I say.

"It's Liam."

"I'm busy."

"It's my time. Ten o'clock."

I pitch my voice at the door like a dagger. "Go." He huffs in frustration but he leaves, and I turn back to Prima and see the look on her face. A look that says, *Are you a queen, or a prisoner?*

And how do I explain it? How do I say, *You know nothing but being valued. You've been special since the day you were born. You don't even know what you're giving up.* How do I explain what it means to be treated with deference and respect, to be an *only* instead of a *many*? To hand a man his newborn son in the one scant corner of the world that still makes sons? If her whole life hasn't taught her that, what can I hope to tell her that will change her mind? What fifteen-year-old wants to take her mother's word for anything?

So instead I say, "All right." She looks surprised, and then relieved. I can see all the tension of the last few months drain out of her. "Stay here tonight," I say, and she nods. We climb into my bed and I kneel beside her and unbraid her hair, run my fingers through to clear the tangles away, blow out the candle. She leans her head against my chest like she used to as a child, and I stroke her hair until she falls asleep.

The next morning I rise early, bathe, and change into my best clothes, a white muslin dress that floats when I walk. I braid my hair and twist it onto the top of my head, then frown at myself in the mirror. Who am I dressing up for? For the MPs, who always judge me with their disapproving stares? Why should I value their opinions more than those of the men I live with every day?

Prima goes to her cabin and returns with the bag of things she'll take with her. Such a small bag. Her boots, the ones I've made, are slung over one shoulder. As we walk to the yard I already hear the approaching rumble of hooves. Too soon, I think. Too fast. I open the gate and the MPs ride in, looking ill at ease on their horses, hands on their guns, as always.

The last woman through the gate leads an empty horse. By now a half dozen of the men have gathered, but most of them are not looking at Prima. They're looking at the MPs, ten adult women all together in one place. The MPs are fit, athletic, young. Some of them are quite beautiful. My eyes sting with jealousy even as the one in charge taps her finger against the grip of her gun, a silent reminder.

Prima and I embrace. "Thank you," she says.

"Be good," I tell her, and kiss her forehead.

She packs her belongings into the saddlebags and begins lashing the boots to the outside of one of them. I try to imagine her wearing those boots with her new clothes, shimmering synthetic dresses or blue jeans or whatever has replaced those things. They'll look like something from another time.

As though she could hear my thoughts, the MP who holds Prima's horse says, "You won't need those. We have better ones in the city."

"No, you don't," says Prima. "My mother made these." She finishes tying them in place. The MP grimaces as though she has tasted something sour but doesn't answer. Prima looks at me and nods. I see pity in her face, and excitement for the life she's heading toward. We've done our job too well. We've made her strong enough to walk away from us all.

"You can come with me," she says. The MPs wait for my reply. But we all know I won't.

"You're not my only child," I tell her, and she nods. This is the easiest answer, a true one, but not the full one. If she *were* my only child, would I go?

I'm about to wish her good luck when a strange expression passes across her face, a mix of pain and confusion. I look behind me and there is Apollo, standing quietly. Prima stands still for a moment, shoulders thrown back as if that could save her. He only smiles softly at her, asks for nothing, and then she is running across the packed dirt of the yard, throwing herself into his arms. He lifts her up to his chest. She wraps her arms around his neck, her legs around his waist, her body shaking with sobs as she buries her face in his shoulder. For a long time he says nothing, just sways her gently back and forth. Then he whispers something in her ear. She nods but keeps crying.

The MPs look away. They're young women, two-egg babies, none of them with a father to remember. But I see, or maybe imagine, a hunger in their faces, the sudden awareness of something they never knew they were missing.

At last Apollo sets Prima on her feet. He leans down and says one more thing to her, something that makes her laugh through her tears. Then he turns her around, back toward the MPs, and sends her forward. How is it that he can be so much more gracious than I am, he who spent more time with her than anyone? Where is his sense of betrayal, of loss? What does he know that I don't? Prima mounts her horse, and turns it toward the gate, and rides off without another word, the MPs falling into line behind her.

That night Apollo comes to me, long past when we should both be asleep. He chimes the bell tentatively, softly enough that I would not hear it if I were not awake, and

I drag the heavy oak beam back along its track and swing the door wide. At the sight of me his face slides into ruin, tears spilling from his eyes even as I take him by the hand. When we have sex tonight, it won't be about physical pleasure or even romance. It'll be about seeking a comfort that can't be found, except in sharing our loss. He has known for years that this day would come. That if she didn't go to the city she would go to another camp to bear other men's children, that she would be lost to him in one way or another. Knowing all this, he could have kept his distance but chose not to. We pull each other closer and I wonder, What can the city offer that is worth all this pain?

An excerpt from

HEAVEN

BY EMERSON WHITNEY

I used to watch Mom on TV, would pull the videos out of the back of the cupboard while I was home sick as a teenager, they were in green VHS sleeves, in the way back. I don't know where they are now and it doesn't matter because nobody has a VCR. A blonde man and woman sat forward in heavy floral chairs. They chatted, glanced at the camera from the foreground of a pastel painting of Sacramento, the woman's shoulder pads blotting out the American River. The woman turned to face the camera, she said Marie.

A craft-scene backdrop slapped onto the screen. A blue wall. The camera panned to Mom behind a brown table filled with scraps of things, paper. She was perfect and '80s, had giant red glasses. She blinked at the camera, held up a cutout of my image that she'd made into a lampshade. I was adorable as a lampshade, was four or something years old.

In the photo Mom was holding, I wore overalls and a pink baseball cap. My hands were in my pockets. I looked a little pissed.

She was saying something about my dad, said *Dad* flatly, and I was surprised to hear it. She showed the audience how to make a calendar for kids to understand visitation when their parents were divorced, she moved the cutout of me to Monday, Wednesday. I never saw Dad like she was talking about, we didn't have a schedule and we didn't live close. She talked about me and explained decoupage, her hair was clipped behind her head, glasses leaning off her nose, beautiful. She made perfect sense.

When the show was live, I'd watch it from a car seat in the living room, I was four, the shadow of a palm tree moving across the floor. I rocked in the car seat with my arms crossed. There was nothing in the room, just foam-green carpet and a bucket of paint at the entry to the kitchen, white paint that smelled empty. I don't know why there was only a car seat.

All those times that Mom's face was center on TV, I waited for her wave. I'd watch her voice, her body, projecting, moving onto its toes. She'd hold her elbow up and smile at the studio audience. I'd wave back. Music would come on, synth-y music about Sacramento, the crush of light in the living room would make the screen too white, her face and her waving would careen off into an advertisement, leave the echo of her voice in the room like paint.

I'd push myself out of the car seat, pad into the kitchen, tip a chair onto its back two legs and drag it toward the refrigerator. I always used the same chair, the one with the loose cushion, tan and wrinkled. I'd hoist myself onto the seat, always an inch or two too short to be eye level with the top, would open the freezer and lodge my foot between the interior racks, and use that fulcrum to pull my pacifier off the fridge, the blue one, the one with the elephant on the tip. They stuck it up there so I'd stop sucking on it. I'd stand on the chair totally triumphant, shove it into my mouth with both hands, smile behind it.

When I was an infant, I'd put my mouth around Mom's actual nipple and my face would fill with snot. A red, pimply ring would grow where my mouth was. I gave Mom mastitis, was allergic to her milk. I was allergic to formula, too, to everything, I coughed.

My younger brothers drank her up, when she'd come into the house, they'd feel her breasts arriving. They'd shriek and run toward her legs. I'd hang back. Her smell would rush at me anyway. Light would shift in the house, Mom's voice flickered against the clicking on of lamps. Here's the etymology:

Mammary is a word that's likely derived from a natural sound in baby talk, perhaps imitative of the sound made while sucking—*ma*. The ache of wanting is enormous. I drank off the plug like a drunk. I'm not ashamed.

Mama is from 1707; *mum* is from 1823; *mummy* in this sense is from 1839; *mommy*, 1844; *momma*, 1852; and *mom*, 1867.

And *mastectomy*, or the surgical removal of a breast, is from 1909, from the Greek *mastos*, like masticate, burn. It's like "the splitting of rocks or gems," from *cleavage*—"the cutting along a fissure line."

I'm thinking about giving an account of myself.

"The stories do not capture the body to which they refer. Even the history of this body is not fully narratable," Judith Butler writes. "Any effort to 'give an account of oneself' will have to fail in order to approach being true."

Here's a clear failure: there's always an urgency around my portrait.

When I had boobs, the dudes I'd get naked with would say, "Wow, so ethnic." I had one guy who'd call them my "Nat Geo boobs." They'd rub their finger across my areola when they said it. It was fucked up and I was proud, too, because everyone told me they came from my grandmother's body. I cut them off years ago now. I don't read the same anymore. In the process, my nipples got spotty, brown and pink, and I shake my shoulders. They're gone into this kind of skin confetti that I don't understand, chewing gum nipples, my friend says, wrinkled and weird. I shut a door.

Now I am not passing. My attempt to write this history falters. Are body parts passed down? Grammy always wants to hand me the negatives of things: she doesn't want me to have kids, she doesn't want me to cook, she tries to toss me a kind of freedom she never had. My maternal line is wives and widows that cleaned banks at night. Grammy wanted to be a cruise ship stewardess and travel, she got married instead. Her inability to retire grates on her—I'm never able to stop cooking lunch for your grandpa, fifty years of lunches and not one day off, she always says and she means every meal every day.

I love this woman for throwing me into deep water. She wants to hoist me up every once in a while and look. My heritage is her hopefulness and the complexity of a body that looks, in parts, like hers.

The last time I visited, Grammy called me to her bedside, she was sitting on the edge of her bed about to take a nap, and she asked me to hand her a plastic CVS bag on the floor—I got you this, she said, rummaging through it. She pulled out a black box with a clear plastic cover, a facial hair remover called Flawless. I don't even know how it does the removing, says it has a built-in LED light: "discreet." There's a full moon on the cover and it boasts an "18-karat gold plated" head. The video on their website says it uses German-engineered technology to fit a hair remover inside a lipstick container. You can use it when "unwanted hairs pop up out of nowhere," the video says. At the end, there's footage of somebody carefully rubbing the lipstick container in circles on a blown-up, peach-colored balloon in a demonstration of gentleness. It honestly looks fun. I didn't want to use it on my face—my toes, maybe, but my chin hairs have been growing forever and I like letting them.

I said thanks, but I like to touch my chin hairs when I think and she laughed and was like, Okay, whatever, like you're so funny. She tugged a second Flawless out of the bag, Got one for myself, too, she said, because she was trying to help.

This is the question of my body and my story about it: Is it just mine? I imagine that these hairs or these boobs are exclusively mine somehow, that the scars or the hairs are unique to me, and it's not true. The only thing I'm doing any different from my grandmother is leaving the hairs there, it's the opposite with the boobs. I could just remove the hairs like I did the boobs, or Grammy and I could together.

I notice a crashing in my chest, the slap of belonging, it's a rocking that dislodges all the time—I want to relate to the clicking in my joints, and the skipping record of my person. I want to relate to it like sounds of people smoking cigarettes on the corner, a lighter flicking on and off, noise like birds, maybe.

I don't particularly like how I look, but this doesn't constitute anything. My thighs meet in a way I find totally objectionable, like a heart with the point as my ankles, though I am satisfied with myself sometimes, and know what beauty feels like when it crosses me, subtle, like folding a quilt.

Really, I can't explain myself without making a mess.

Butler goes on to suggest that we've always already failed at giving this account of ourselves in part because we didn't ask for the language we use (the one or several that we've had to shuffle ourselves into) or the condition of being addressed in that language, and so we're already lacking control from the start.

Similarly, no one asked for the framework of male and female or the aggregate of gender that we're funneled through. I wonder all the time how much of my identity is influenced by woman-ness or attempts at woman-ness and the way it was passed to me. We're all handed a responsibility. Here's gender: "woman" as a category is fraught, and entire groups have been denied access. "Could we, in fact, release the category of woman from its fixity and white normativity?" writes Saidiya V. Hartman about "the name 'woman'" and what it "designate[s]," in *Scenes of Subjection*.

I'm interested in what genderqueer Korean American artist and writer Johanna Hedva suggests in their writing on womanhood and disability. Hedva expands the meaning of "woman" to include all oppressed peoples ("the un-cared for, the secondary, the oppressed, the non-, the un-, the less-than") because as it stands, the term doesn't suffice. In their article "Sick Woman Theory," published in *Mask Magazine*, Hedva writes that "the identity of 'woman' has erased and excluded many (especially women of color and trans and genderfluid people)."

The photo accompanying the article shows a gathered-up Hedva in a flowing red dress, black lipstick, black beads, pill bottles billowing out from underneath one arm. In Hedva's alternate use of the word, *woman* functions as "a strategic, all-encompassing embrace."

Hedva lets the word, like any word, move around. *Woman* doesn't mean a body.

You know, I was going through my things the other day and I found a photo of you that looked just like Ingrid Bergman, my grandma said a few visits ago. She shook her head. I had to look at it twice, you looked just like Ingrid Bergman.

You're biased, I said, I'm just symmetrical.

She laughed, hung her elbows off the end of the bed. She looked down at the carpet, moved it with her toe.

I was staying in this room that is really a closet-sized space attached to hers. Every night before bed, she'd change into a nightgown then come into my room, lean against my bed, hang her arms off the frame. She would chat with me before I went to sleep.

I'm thirty-three. This is still routine. I knotted the covers over the emptiness in my chest and smiled, afraid that she'd try to tuck me in and brush the lack in my clinging sleep T-shirt, wonder where my boobs went. I haven't told her and it's been almost ten years.

As a kid, I'd play with the bigness of her biceps, fascinated by how it swung. I'd hug her and fall into her cleavage, called her Boobers. She called me Boobettes as soon as mine grew. This was our bond. No one else in the family had her eyes and no one else had her boobs, I don't know why anyone thought it was appropriate to make this a topic of conversation, but it regularly was. I'd curl my shoulders in to make them less of a thing. I only brought my shoulders back around Grammy, all proud.

At the end of my bed, Grammy looked like everything about me, older. I loved her there, pinching my toes, talking to me like she used to when I lived with her, first as an infant for a few years, and then again for three years starting from the time I was eight. She adjusted my quilt. There were cars braking and moving outside, a line of summer cars headed to hotels. The room smelled like baby powder and warm vacuum, clean carpet. Night was always lit by her snores. I readied for her breath.

I was wondering, Grammy said, looking up at me. Have you ever wondered... I mean, do you think you're like this because your mom likes your brothers more?

My feet tightened. She looked at me with our eyes, a thudding green, everyone else's are brown or blue. In there was so much worry, a wealth of earnest worry as she hung her arms over the end of the bed. She'd been frustrated with me about stereotypical things, she didn't like that I wore baggy clothes or wanted a men's scarf once as a gift. She's not all that femme-presenting herself, so my sense was that whatever she'd been told to do, she was telling me too. We had a tradition of dissecting our family's relationships, she and I spent so much time alone over the years and we'd process. Grammy asking about my brothers was a gesture like checking the engine, she'd stuck the metal rod in the oil and pulled it out, was looking at the level aloud with me. She tightened her mouth when she was done looking and nodded. This is how I took it: your mom fucked up and that fuckup made you you.

I took a breath. She said, I don't know why I asked. Don't worry about it, it's time for bed.

I won't be able to sleep, I figured.

Her arm swished as she pinched my toe. I love you, she said, walking toward the door. She paused with her hand on it, looked back at me.

THE
LIVES AND
THOUGHTS
OF A
FREE PEOPLE

REVISITING A FEW
HISTORIC ACLU CASES

Excerpted from *Fight of the Century: Writers Reflect on 100 Years of Landmark ACLU Cases*, edited by Michael Chabon and Ayelet Waldman

SCOTTSBORO, USA: A BRIEF HISTORY

BY JACQUELINE WOODSON

Powell v. Alabama (1932)

Patterson v. Alabama (1935)

In 1931, nine black American teenagers hopped on an Alabama train headed toward Chattanooga, Tennessee. Later called the Scottsboro Boys, they were named Haywood Patterson, Clarence Norris, Charlie Weems, Andy Wright, Roy Wright, Olen Montgomery, Ozie Powell, Willie Roberson, and Eugene Williams. When two white women falsely accused these black men of rape, all men were arrested and imprisoned.

What followed was a quintessential example of

American injustice. The Scottsboro Boys were not allowed to speak with an attorney prior to trial, and a lynch mob encircled the jail that held them. When they finally met their two court-appointed lawyers, the Scottsboro Boys discovered them to be ill prepared for trial and completely unfamiliar with the case. One was actually an intoxicated volunteer from the trial's audience. Unnerved by the publicity and thousands of potentially violent onlookers, the trial judge rushed the cases through his docket. Over the course of two and a half days, a series of all-white juries sentenced all nine teenagers to death, despite the clear ineffectiveness of their counsel, the frenetic proceedings, and the complete lack of evidence that any rape had occurred, much less been committed by the Scottsboro Boys. The mere allegation of sexual relations with a white woman was sufficient to condemn them.

The Communist Party USA sponsored the appeal and provided counsel in what would become *Powell v. Alabama*. Recognizing the need for experienced counsel, the ACLU's Walter Pollak was retained to argue that the Scottsboro Boys' hasty trial and nominal legal counsel violated the Fourteenth Amendment's due process clause. The US Supreme Court agreed. Justice George Sutherland wrote that criminal defendants in capital cases are constitutionally entitled to legal counsel. However, mere presence of counsel is not enough. Due process demanded that court-appointed counsel be effective, well versed in the case, and prepared to protect the defendant's freedom. After this initial victory, two additional appeals were required, *Norris v. Alabama* and *Patterson v. Alabama*. In both, Pollak and the ACLU contested Alabama's systematic exclusion of black Americans from the jury pool based solely on their race. In a major victory, the court agreed that such discrimination was unconstitutional.

This legal triumph, however, has a bittersweet ending. Charges were eventually dropped against four of the Scottsboro Boys, and they returned home after years of incarceration. The remaining five were convicted, despite one of the white women recanting her testimony and admitting the entire story of rape was a lie. Including pretrial detention, each served at least a decade in prison for a crime that never even existed.

* * *

The youngest was thirteen. The oldest, twenty. Decades later, when the Scottsboro Boys' musical came to Broadway, I began to cough as the actors smiled and danced their way through the play. I coughed as I turned to see the pleased faces of the white audience. I coughed as they clapped along and cheered. Coughed through the blackface on black faces. Through the minstrel show. I coughed so hard

I had to leave the theater, and minutes later, I couldn't stop coughing. Returned later to cough from my seat through the standing ovation.

It's a response to stress, the coughing is. For as long as I can remember, my own body has told me to remember to breathe as it prevented me from doing so. Breathe. No don't. Breathe. No don't. Has told me, through the gagging spasms, that the moment I'm moving through is triggering. Call it genetic memory. Call it the curse of DNA. Call it America. Call it a country that makes black and breathing nearly impossible.

Please don't tell what train I'm on... Call it a song by Elizabeth Cotten. Call it cotton.

Before someone white decided to turn a black tragedy into music and dance for two hundred dollars a seat and no intermission, there were nine brown boys leaving Alabama. Olen, at seventeen, was nearly blind.

Think Blind Boys of Alabama. Think Huck Finn.

Think Trayvon Martin.

Think the broken promise of forty acres and a mule, Jim Crow, the Great Depression, the big black brute, the white damsel in distress, the American dream—

Think strange fruit hanging from poplar trees.

Think Amos and Andy. Think Toms, Coons, Mulattos, Mammies and Bucks and—

The first movie we watched in my African Americans

in Film course in college was *The Birth of a Nation*. Before *Cabin in the Sky* with the beautiful Lena Horne. Before Fredi Washington graced the screen in *Imitation of Life*, there was D. W. Griffith's gaze on America.

By then, four of the Scottsboro Boys were already walking, two were suckling infants, and Ozie, Eugene, and Leroy hadn't yet been born.

In February 2008, my son was born. We named him Jackson Leroi. Think twenty-two sophomores and freshmen. All of us knowing how black and blue we were at our small liberal arts PWI. With no BSU. Far away from any HBCU. It was the mid-1980s. We had Anita Baker, Luther Vandross, and a professor with an Afro named Dr. Jackson getting us through. But by then, my hair was permanently straightened, and when I left my African Americans in Film class, there was my all-white cheerleading team. There was my all-white dorm and white boyfriend. There was my all-white major of English literature, my all-white minor—British Lit. A year later, there would be my all-black sorority. A year later, I would learn about nine black boys. And as the years bent into decades, I would call out their names. The youngest one, brown-skinned and baby-faced, was named Leroy. Andy, Clarence, and Charlie were the oldest. And between them there were Haywood, Olen, and Ozie.

And baby-faced Leroy was leaving home for the first

time. Olen, who was nearly blind. His dream—a pair of glasses.

This wasn't in the musical. The story of a boy so blind he had to leave home, steal a ride on a train with the hopes of a job. With the hopes of one day seeing.

How do we begin to tell this country's story without turning our own selves inside out?

In 1992, my college boyfriend died from the complications of AIDS. I was living on Cape Cod by then. By then, I had long cut off the damaged processed hair of my college days and grown it back as locks. When I remembered college, I remembered *The Birth of a Nation* and Dr. Jackson and the dividing line between the many white cheerleaders and the three black ones.

In an article that ran in *Life* magazine (1937), Eugene was described as a "sullen, shifty mulatto." What thirteen-year-old isn't sullen?

Mulatto: the term may derive from *mula* (current Portuguese word, from the Latin *mūlus*), meaning "mule, the hybrid offspring of a horse and a donkey."

I know I know: don't trust Wiki. Whatever.

Remember Leroy? Here's an excerpt of the letter he wrote to his mama: "I am all lonely and thinking of you…

I feel like I can eat some of your cooking Mom." Some sources say he was twelve. Some thirteen.

But the boys were from Scottsboro. And this is America.

And the truth is never where it's supposed to be. So shucks, y'all.

Let's all just keep smiling and dancing. Smiling and dancing.

YOU'VE GIVEN ME A LOT TO THINK ABOUT

BY CHARLIE JANE ANDERS

Schroer v. Billington (2008)

In 2004, the Library of Congress rescinded Diane Schroer's job offer on learning that she was in the process of transitioning from male to female. In *Schroer v. Billington*, the ACLU, acting as Schroer's counsel, urged the court to find that the library's actions violated Title VII, which prohibits employment discrimination on the basis of sex. Despite multiple appellate courts' prior refusals to find statutory protection for trans employees, the court agreed with the ACLU, holding that the library's actions amounted to impermissible sex stereotyping, as well as to a violation of the most literal reading of the text of

Title VII. Schroer was awarded the maximum damages allowed, marking a significant personal victory and a deeper societal understanding of what it means to be protected from discrimination on the basis of sex.

*   *   *

Five days before Christmas 2004, Diane Schroer went to the Library of Congress to talk to her new boss. I picture it being one of those ugly DC winters, where the cold air from the Potomac stings your cheeks and gets inside your winter clothes. Schroer must have been doubly uncomfortable, because she was wearing men's clothing that no longer felt right. A twenty-five-year decorated veteran, Schroer had just been hired to work at the Congressional Research Service, and she was here to come out as a transgender woman.

Schroer was already midtransition but hadn't yet legally changed her name or gender marker, which is why she'd interviewed for the job under her assigned-at-birth name. And she already had facial feminization surgery scheduled before the job was supposed to begin. She explained all of this to the CRS's Charlotte Preece, who took in all this information and then just said, "You've given me a lot to think about." Preece immediately set about the process of pulling the plug on Schroer's job offer, on the (probably bogus) theory that Schroer would need a whole new security clearance as "Diane" rather than keeping the security clearance she'd already obtained under her old name. Preece also felt that Schroer would be distracted by transitioning, plus both Schroer's old military contacts and Congress might not take her seriously as a trans woman.

Preece told Schroer, "You are putting me and CRS in an awkward position." With the help of the ACLU, Schroer sued the CRS for job discrimination—and won, helping to reinforce that trans people are protected under Title VII's prohibitions on sex discrimination. This was a big deal, because some other high-profile cases (like *Ulane v. Eastern Airlines*, 1984) had gone the opposite way, with judges insisting that Title VII applied only to people being discriminated against for their assigned-at-birth gender.

In *Schroer v. Billington*, Judge James Robertson dismissed all of the security concerns and other issues as "pretextual." And he held that discrimination against trans people was "sex stereotyping," similar to the famous case of *Price Waterhouse v. Hopkins* (1989), where a female employee was discriminated against for being insufficiently feminine. He also held that discriminating against someone because that person is transitioning from one sex to another is necessarily sex discrimination prohibited by Title VII. (Robertson compares this situation to a recent convert from Christianity to Judaism facing religious discrimination.)

A few years after *Schroer*, in 2011, the ACLU won another major victory for trans people, striking down a Wisconsin law, the Inmate Sex Change Prevention Act, which prohibited the use of any state funds to treat trans prisoners with hormones or surgery. Wisconsin argued that because prisons were providing antidepressants and counseling to trans prisoners, the law should stand. But an appeals court ruled that this would be similar to giving painkillers and therapy to cancer patients and calling it a day.

When I started to transition, I knew the law wasn't on my side. California hadn't yet passed a law protecting trans people from discrimination, and the courts were spitting out rulings like *Ulane v. Eastern Airlines* all the time. If I wanted to rent an apartment, get a job, or even just walk on the street in peace, I had to depend on the enlightened goodwill of others. Even now, trans and nonbinary people (especially people of color) have much higher rates of unemployment and homelessness and have much worse access to health care and other services.

I was turned down for a couple of jobs explicitly for being trans. (In both cases, they had told me over the phone that I had the job, and then they met me in person, and suddenly I had given them a lot to think about.) I was turned down for health insurance, too, because being trans was a "preexisting condition."

So victories like *Schroer* matter a lot. It matters that

employers and prisons will think twice before discriminating against trans people—but also the reasons for these rulings matter. Judge Robertson's ruling in *Schroer* calls out other judges who had ruled that Title VII couldn't include trans people for having too narrow a view of the statute's intent (quoting, of all people, Antonin Scalia, as propounding an expansive view of sex discrimination).

Back in the day, the ACLU was fighting just for people to appear in public in clothes that were at odds with their assigned gender—because even having a gender-nonconforming appearance was often illegal under local "cross-dressing" ordinances. And according to ACLU attorney Chase Strangio, these cases were usually fought on the grounds of "free speech" and "due process" rather than sex discrimination.

For example, in 1985, the ACLU of Hawaii intervened on behalf of a group of LGBTQAI+ people who wanted to hold a Miss Gay Molokai pageant featuring contestants in drag. Some local churches objected, and Maui County mayor Hannibal Tavares decided to ban the pageant, calling it "unwholesome and inappropriate." But the ACLU fought Tavares in court and won. (The ACLU attorney in this case, Dan Foley, later won same-sex marriage rights in Hawaii and went on to become a judge.)

I can't imagine living in a world where I could be arrested just for being in a dress despite the label a doctor slapped on me when I was born. Or where a harmless drag show could be outlawed. (In the Miss Gay Molokai case, people expressed a concern that the mere existence of a drag performance on the island "might spread AIDS.") But I also can't believe that in my lifetime, there was a moment when my identity as a trans woman could only have been defended as a free speech issue—as if I'm making some kind of a point or trying to express something. It's not enough for me to exist; I have to be saying something. And if my gender presentation is a form of speech, then I'm clearly giving people a lot to think about just by occupying physical space.

In the 1990s and early 2000s, the ACLU started taking on more cases involving people being disciplined at work for "being gender-nonconforming," says Strangio, plus more cases about student rights and employment discrimination. And the ACLU increased its already-strong focus on the rights of trans prisoners. But it wasn't until the past several years that the ACLU has been pursuing more sex discrimination cases involving trans plaintiffs.

And now that the federal government is trying to erase trans people in as many ways as possible—making it easier to deny us health care, keeping us from serving in the military, allowing discrimination based on religion, and even working to define gender as based on "biological sex"—these fights are even more important than before.

And that's why I'm proud to be a supporter of the ACLU.

I'm not here to give you a lot to think about. My body is not a statement, or an inconvenience, or a threat to anyone's security. My gender isn't a mistake, or a disruption, or a rebellion against biology, and I don't need anybody's tolerance for my self-expression. Put simply, this is about bodies and personhood and trans people's right to live our lives. When some bodies are illegal, when people are forced to choose either having basic rights or being their authentic selves, then everybody is diminished.

Trans and nonbinary people have only recently been recognized as having basic rights, and we'll have to fight to keep them. But when those battles come, at least we'll be standing on high ground, thanks to the valiance and dedication of those who came before us.

LEGAL COUNSEL AT THE MOMENT MOST CRUCIAL

BY DAVE EGGERS

Escobedo v. Illinois (1964)

In *Escobedo v. Illinois*, the ACLU of Illinois brought suit on behalf of a man convicted of murder largely based on a statement he made alone while subjected to police questioning. Although the lower courts dealt with the case primarily in terms of settled Fifth Amendment tests of voluntariness, the Supreme Court, in an opinion written by Justice Arthur Goldberg, chose instead for the first time to extend Sixth Amendment "assistance of counsel" protections to an accused person under police interrogation. This 5–4 split decision built on *Gideon v. Wainwright* (1963) to make such statements inadmissible

> due to denial of attorney assistance, a principle that was
> later advanced by *Miranda v. Arizona* (1966).

* * *

On the night of January 19, 1960, Manuel Valtierra
was murdered in Chicago. The police suspected that his
brother-in-law, Danny Escobedo, might have pulled the
trigger, given that Escobedo's sister, Grace, claimed that
Valtierra had abused her. Escobedo was arrested a few hours
after the shooting and was brought in for questioning. He
said nothing substantial to the police and was released that
day. On January 30, Benedict DiGerlando, also a suspect
in the killing, told the police that Escobedo had fired the
fatal shots, and Escobedo was brought in again on that day.

Once at the precinct, Escobedo told the police that he
wanted his lawyer, Warren Wolfson, present during any
interrogation. The police refused. Escobedo's mother called
Wolfson, notifying him of Escobedo's arrest. Wolfson
arrived at the precinct and made his presence known to
the sergeant on duty. The sergeant refused to allow him
to see Escobedo. At one point, Wolfson caught sight of
Escobedo as he was being interrogated, but police still
did not grant him the right to speak to his client until,
they said, they "were done" with him. Meanwhile, during
the interrogation, Escobedo repeatedly asked to have his

counsel present, but police told him that Wolfson did not want to see him. During their interrogation of Escobedo, detectives extracted what they claimed was a confession, and at trial, Escobedo was convicted of murder.

Escobedo appealed this conviction, and the case wound its way to the Supreme Court, with Bernard Weisberg arguing for the ACLU with Walter T. Fisher. The court decided, 5–4, in Escobedo's favor, noting that the Constitution guarantees a defendant the right to a lawyer, and that thwarting that right during interrogation defeats the entire purpose of that right. "The guiding hand of counsel," the court wrote, was most crucial at this most delicate part of the criminal justice process. In the end, the conviction was overturned and the precedent in *Escobedo v. Illinois*, decided in 1964, established the right of any suspect to have a lawyer present during police questioning. In its ruling, made in the thick of the Cold War, the court also noted that "the Soviet criminal code does not permit a lawyer to be present during an investigation. The Soviet trial has thus been aptly described as 'an appeal from the pretrial investigation.'"

Escobedo v. Illinois brought necessary progress that improved the criminal justice system. A few years later, *Miranda v. Arizona* established what we now know as our Miranda rights, which must be read to anyone being arrested prior to questioning and which include the right to remain silent and the right to an attorney. *Miranda* built on, and in a way supplanted, *Escobedo*. Thereafter, not only did a suspect have a right to an attorney during interrogation, but police had to inform the suspect of these rights during the arrest. All of this was positive and long overdue.

And yet.

And yet we still have widespread, even epidemic problems with forced confessions. According to the Innocence Project, one out of every four defendants whose convictions was later overturned using DNA evidence were originally convicted through a false or forced confession. And the problem is diabolical. Even when innocent suspects know their rights, they often agree to answer questions without an attorney present *because they know they are innocent*. They want to be helpful. They feel they have nothing to hide. And they don't want to appear guilty by hiring a lawyer.

And thus they answer questions and are frequently tricked or pressured into a confession. Sometimes they're interrogated so long—on average, interrogations last sixteen hours—that they'll say anything to leave the room and go to sleep. Sometimes detectives simply lie to them, claiming evidence they actually don't have, or they fabricate witnesses who implicate them in the crime. And then there are the instances of force, or the threat of force, and the instances of the suspect being too young or otherwise mentally unable to understand the nature of an interrogation and the gravity of what might be self-incrimination.

Culturally, we have to change our thinking about interrogations. Every police procedural on television and film glamorizes these interrogations and implicitly approves of what are undeniable human abuses and violations of the Constitution. Suspects are kept chained to chairs, are denied food and water, are kept under hot lights, and are pitted against friends and family. They are deceived and intimidated. They are told that their conviction is assured and that their punishment will be far worse unless they confess. And all the while, audiences are expected to approve because the detectives, certain of the suspect's guilt, simply need to get to the desired result, conviction, with a minimum of interference. This makes for good and satisfying entertainment but represents a fundamental misunderstanding of the rights of suspects in a free society.

As a nation, we still, nearly sixty years after *Escobedo v. Illinois*, look askance at anyone who asks for an attorney before speaking with police. We still see this as some kind of admission of guilt. Why would an innocent person need a lawyer? we ask. This attitude must change. Waiting until an attorney is present must be seen as an act of wisdom—an acknowledgment of the wisdom of the Sixth and Fourteenth Amendments—rather than as evidence of guilt.

And after we achieve that, we have more changes ahead: all interrogations must be electronically recorded to be valid; interrogations must be limited to a reasonable amount of time (a study by the Center on Wrongful Convictions and the University of California, Irvine, found that 84 percent of false confessions occurred after interrogations of more than six hours); and interrogators must be prohibited from lying to suspects—presenting false evidence, false witnesses, and false scenarios involving leniency if the suspect confesses.

We have a ways to go to make the system better and to prevent the towering moral offense of wrongful conviction. But *Escobedo* was a landmark case that no doubt prevented thousands of innocent men and women from being railroaded into self-incrimination. "We have learned the lesson of history, ancient and modern," Justice Goldberg wrote in the majority opinion, "that a system of criminal law enforcement which comes to depend on the 'confession' will, in the long run, be less reliable and more subject to abuse than a system which depends on extrinsic evidence independently secured through skillful investigation."

BECAUSE GIRLS CAN READ AS WELL AS BOYS:

ON PROTECTING THE CHILDREN

BY NEIL GAIMAN

Reno v. ACLU (1997)

Ashcroft v. ACLU (2004)

Reno v. ACLU and *Ashcroft v. ACLU* are quintessential First Amendment cases. The federal government deemed a given form of speech socially harmful and took steps to silo it away. In *Reno*, the court ruled that the Communications Decency Act's definition of *obscenity* was too broad and imprecise, censoring an enormous swath of otherwise legal speech, and therefore fell afoul of the First Amendment. In *Ashcroft*, the court struck down the Child Online Protection Act (COPA) as overbroad and ill tailored to its purpose, and therefore also unconstitutional.

In both cases, the ACLU shouldered the burden of making uncomfortable arguments in order to protect free speech, and adhered to its higher principles in fighting to protect a core American freedom from overzealous legislators.

* * *

Two weeks before I was born, in October 1960, D. H. Lawrence's novel *Lady Chatterley's Lover* was put on trial for obscenity.

It was a jury trial, and at the end of it, the book was found not to be obscene. I was born on the day the book, in its cheap paperback edition, went on sale (and sold out, all across the United Kingdom). Mervyn Griffith-Jones, the prosecutor, had asked the jury in his opening statement, "When you have read it through, would you approve of your young sons, young daughters—because girls can read as well as boys—reading this book? Is it a book that you would have lying around in your own house? Is it a book that you would even wish your wife or your servants to read?" Normally, only the last sentence of this is quoted, making fun of the antiquated attitudes of lawyers who had failed to realize that the '60s were just about to happen and sexual intercourse was, as Philip Larkin put it, about to begin: after all, wives in 1960 were allowed to choose

244

their own reading material, and the servant classes were being replaced by labor-saving devices.

The question that hangs in the air, though, always, and that colors conversation of censorship is the first half of Griffith-Jones's question: Would you approve of your young sons, or your young daughters, reading this book, seeing this image, being exposed to this idea?

As adults, one of our responsibilities is to protect children. Some of this protection takes the form of keeping children away from images, from ideas, from stories, from films that we do not feel they are ready for.

Not all adults agree on the boundaries of this protective sphere, and not all children are the same. And "children" is a slippery concept, defined differently in different places. Where does childhood end? Would you protect a six-year-old from the same ideas or images you would protect a seventeen-and-a-half-year-old from? And how do "community standards," the nebulous but still legally real idea that different people in different places have different views on what is or isn't acceptable, fit into all this?

We want to protect our children. But legal arguments, like the one made in the *Lady Chatterley's Lover* case, presume something about children that is not actually true: they assume that children read and parse fiction that contains sex in the same way that adults do.

Children want to know things. They are curious. But

they tend to explore within their comfort zone.

Children are good at exploring and pretty good at figuring out their comfort zones. On the whole, they would tend not to pick up horror fiction, or even go to Judy Blume to learn about sex, before they are ready. But when they are ready and curious, they explore. It's how they make sense of the adult world waiting for them. And children will make mistakes in their exploration. They will go too far. I remember waiting for my mother as a boy, and, bored, picking up the only reading material around, which turned out to be a well-documented, respectable, illustrated publication about murder methods in World War II concentration camps and Nazi experiments on human subjects who were mostly, like me, Jewish. I had known we had lost many relatives: discovering how, and discovering how human beings could kill other human beings, became the stuff of my nightmares.

(Quick! Define *children*. At what age does childhood end? In 2007, a Florida appeals court upheld the successful prosecution of a sixteen-year-old girl and a seventeen-year-old boy as sex offenders, in this case as "child pornographers," for taking photographs of themselves naked and "engaged in sexual activity" [something they were legally of age to do] because the girl had emailed the photos to the boy as keepsakes. Should they have been prosecuted? Should the prosecution have been upheld? And if they had wanted to search the internet for information on how to have sex safely, or for birth control, or even for legal advice on whether it was safe to take naked photos of themselves with their phones, should this have been forbidden or encouraged?)

I write for children. I write for small children. They like destruction and creepy things; they like small journeys into the dark that end safely. I write for older children, who like stories about families and about death and danger. I write for adults. In writing for adults, I always find myself writing, in whatever disguise, about sex and about death. Writing for children, I try and write about hope and the complexity of the world, about bravery and doing the right thing. But there is always death present in the stories. I leave out the sex, because younger children tend to respond to sex in fiction in the way that children respond to a drunk adult throwing up in the street: there's curiosity there, but also aversion, the knowledge that this is part of an adult world that is inevitably waiting for them but is filled with weird-ass things that adults inexplicably do. But several of my adult novels have been honored as adult books that older children would or should read, and they have sex in them, and darkness.

There will always be curiosity about the adult world. There will always be ways to explore that. (I was twelve or thirteen when William Peter Blatty's *The Exorcist* went around the school, passed from hand to hand, from boy to boy. The page with the crucifix masturbation, just like the pages in the unabridged class dictionary that contained the swearwords, was the page the book fell open to.)

The internet began as a place where government employees and academics could exchange information with one another. And then it grew, unplanned and, for the most part, unregulated. The internet is a delivery system. It can deliver a *Batman* cartoon or a porn video. It can deliver tweets or blogs or ads, money or movies or gardening tips. It can offer you all the world's information, or most of it, entertainment and violence, delights and dangers of all kinds. Anything you can encounter in the world outside you can find a version of on the internet. So the question becomes: How do you regulate something so huge, so slippery, so potentially filled with pitfalls? And how do we protect our children from everything in the world? Our six-year-olds as well as our seventeen-and-a-half-year-olds?

As a parent, I want to keep my children safe from all dangers and threats. (I put my hands over my twelve-year-old daughter's eyes during *Pan's Labyrinth*, during the bloody bits, and told her what the subtitles were saying. She didn't want to stop watching, but she didn't want or need the images of blood in her head. But it would have been a lesser film if Guillermo del Toro had been forced to take those moments out of his movie, eliding the adult content to protect the children.)

And governments, responding to that impulse, took the simplest option. They tried, when the internet became a thing, to make the internet a place that would be safe for children.

The way we most often try to codify an official response to large and unruly questions is to fence them in with laws. The first significant attempt by the US government was through Title V of the Telecommunications Act of 1996, better known as the Communications Decency Act (CDA). It was signed into law by President Clinton in 1996 and attempted to target indecency and obscenity on the internet by making it a crime punishable by two years in jail, a $250,000 fine, or both, to engage in speech that was "indecent" or "patently offensive," if that speech could be viewed by a minor.

Within five months, a panel of three judges in Philadelphia had blocked part of the CDA. In July 1997, a federal court in New York struck down a further section, arguing that its reach was too broad. This culminated in *Reno v. ACLU* (1997), in which twenty plaintiffs, including groups representing cyberspace rights and gay and lesbian rights, and the ACLU, challenged the act on the grounds that its provisions would criminalize expression protected by the First Amendment—and specifically that the terms *indecent* and *patently offensive* were both vague and constitutionally overbroad. The Supreme Court agreed, and a landmark 7–2 opinion delivered by Justice John Paul Stevens firmly ruled that the CDA placed an "unacceptably heavy burden on protected speech" that "threatens to torch a large segment of the Internet community."

"The interest in encouraging freedom of expression in a democratic society outweighs any theoretical but unproven benefit of censorship," wrote the court. "We presume government regulation of the content of speech is more likely to interfere with the free exchange of ideas than to encourage it."

The government tried again. In 1998, Congress introduced COPA. It criminalized the posting on the internet, for "commercial purposes," of material that was "harmful to minors," to the tune of a fifty thousand dollar fine and six months in prison. It defined material that was harmful to minors as:

any **communication, picture, image, graphic image file, article, recording, writing, or other matter of any kind that is obscene** or that—

(A) **the average person, applying contemporary community standards,** would find, taking the material as a whole and with respect to minors, is designed to appeal to, or is designed to pander to, the prurient interest;

(B) **depicts, describes, or represents,** in a manner patently offensive with respect to minors, **an actual or simulated sexual act or sexual contact, an actual or simulated normal or perverted sexual act, or a lewd exhibition of the genitals or post-pubescent female breast;** and

(C) taken as a whole, lacks serious literary, artistic, political, or scientific value for minors.

Immediate and obvious problems with this (apart from the oddness of the word *simulated*, which puts a photograph of an oil painting of a naked woman into the same category as a photograph of a naked woman) would be that in applying "community standards" to the entire internet, the most conservative and restrictive communities in the United States would be able to set the standard for everywhere else, in the United States or in the rest of the world. "Community standards" change from place to place, but any of the communities in any of those places could object to what they saw, and the internet would bow to the most restrictive and the most easily upset. And there is always someone, somewhere, who will object to something.

COPA left "for commercial purposes" vague; even if a website is not obviously selling you something, it can still exist for commercial purposes. And what if it is trying to inform you? COPA could have criminalized gyneco-logical websites, websites with information about sexually transmitted diseases, sexual advice columns, and art history sites. It would have meant that adults would have needed to input credit card information before accessing any "commercial" website with adult content, including LGBT information, causing privacy issues (and ignoring the possibility that people under age eighteen can have, or obtain, credit card numbers). And above all, it tried to apply local law to the internet, which is not local: adult content is not found only on US websites.

The case went back and forth between the Third Circuit and the Supreme Court from 2002 until 2009, when the Supreme Court declined to hear the third appeal, effectively striking COPA from the books.

Ashcroft v. ACLU (2004), which ended COPA, was a landmark case. It upheld the injunction, predominantly on the grounds that there were less restrictive ways of tackling the issues than the ones that COPA was attempting to put in place. Justice Anthony Kennedy delivered the majority opinion, explaining that "content-based prohibitions, enforced by severe criminal penalties, have the constant potential to be a repressive force in the lives and thoughts of a free people."

(Though *Ashcroft v. ACLU* is the more recent and more often cited, it is intimately entwined with *Reno v. ACLU*, and observations from the latter cut to the bottom line over the debate on online restrictions. Justice Stevens's majority opinion in 1997 argued that "the interest in encouraging freedom of expression in a democratic society outweighs any theoretical but unproven benefit of censorship.")

Justice Kennedy also pointed out that "the factual record does not reflect current technological reality—a serious flaw in any case involving the Internet. The technology of the Internet evolves at a rapid pace."

As we've seen from attempts by legislators in both the United States and other countries to understand the influence of social media on the 2016 election, this remains a critical issue, and one that's not going to be solved any day soon. COPA's attempt to criminalize pornography and sexual content on commercial sites hosted in the United States would have been powerless in a world where users (including children) could simply jump the fence into the big wide world. Nobody is an island in cyberspace, and no country is either. Even islands aren't really islands any longer. The people who make our laws are always one step behind this new realm they're trying to control, with its strange and flexible geographies.

Overreaching attempts to protect the rights of some are bound to have an adverse impact on the freedoms of others. A recent example has been Tumblr's 2018 decision to ban pornography from its platform, incensing a number of users (including young people, sex workers, and members of the LGBT community) who had relied on it as a relatively safe space for interaction.

Which brings us back to where we came in: the attempt to ban books like *Lady Chatterley's Lover* in order to protect children. The decisions in both *Reno* and *Ashcroft* make explicit reference to the rights of adults, the former in part decided on the grounds that the CDA was an abridgment of the First Amendment because it didn't allow parents to decide what material was acceptable for their children. In 2007, Senior Judge Lowell A. Reed Jr. of the Federal District Court, in a decision that the Supreme Court declined to hear or to overturn, stated that "despite my personal regret at having to set aside yet another attempt to protect our children from harmful material," he was blocking COPA because "perhaps we do the minors of this country harm if First Amendment protections, which they will with age inherit fully, are chipped away in the name of their protection." Children live in a world of adults, and they, in their turn, will become adults one day. We do not and we cannot protect children from the adult world by making the adult world a place safe or fit only for children, and the internet is, for good and for evil, a part of the world, the world as represented by information. As adults, we owe it to our children to protect them, yes. As a positive thing: through communication, by choosing and permitting, as best we can, strictly or permissively, what they encounter in the world, on screens, and on pages. We have to talk to them, inform them, have the awkward and embarrassing conversations we might rather avoid but that are necessary if they are going to navigate the adult waters ahead of them. It's our responsibility to do that.

We do it by helping our children to grow and to learn. We do it by letting them explore and by setting the bounds of their exploration ourselves. We do it by helping them. We don't do it—we can't do it—by removing the adult books from the shelves of a library and by trying to make the whole world into a nursery. If we do, we will find ourselves scraping away the freedoms of the adults who will come after us in our attempts to protect the children they are now.